# Biblical Prophets from A to Z

# Biblical Prophets from A to Z

Known and Unknown

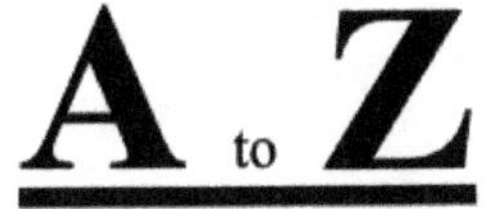


MARK G. BOYER

RESOURCE *Publications* · Eugene, Oregon

BIBLICAL PROPHETS FROM A TO Z
Known and Unknown



Resource Publications
An Imprint of Wipf and Stock Publishers
199 W. 8th Ave., Suite 3
Eugene, OR 97401

www.wipfandstock.com

PAPERBACK ISBN: 979-8-3852-6658-6
HARDCOVER ISBN: 979-8-3852-6659-3
EBOOK ISBN: 979-8-3852-6660-9

VERSION NUMBER 012026

Dedicated to

Victor H. Matthews,

professor emeritus of Religious Studies
and dean emeritus of
the College of Humanities and Public Affairs,
Missouri State University;
author of many books,
endorser of many books,
academic friend.

Life goes not in a straight line . . . , but in a circle.
The first half we spend venturing
as far as the world's end
from home and kin and stillness,
and the latter half
brings us back,
by roundabout ways
but surely to that state from which we set out.

—Cadfael, Peters, *Summer*

# Biblical Prophets A to Z

# Contents

# Abbreviations

BCE = Before the Common Era (same as BC = Before Christ)

**Bibles**

NRSVue = New Revised Standard Version Updated Edition
TM = The Message: Catholic/Ecumenical Edition

**CB (NT) = Christian Bible (New Testament)**

Acts = Acts of the Apostles
1 Cor = First Letter of Paul to the Corinthians
Eph = Letter to the Ephesians
Gal = Letter of Paul to the Galatians
Heb = Letter to the Hebrews
John = John's Gospel
1 John = First Letter of John
Jude = Letter of Jude
Luke = Luke's Gospel
Mark = Mark's Gospel
Matt = Matthew's Gospel
1 Pet = First Letter of Peter
2 Pet = Second Letter of Peter
Rev = Revelation
Rom = Letter of Paul to the Romans

CE = Common Era (same as AD = *Anno Domini*, in the year of the Lord)

**HB (OT) = Hebrew Bible (Old Testament)**

Amos = Amos
1 Chr = First Book of Chronicles
2 Chr = Second Book of Chronicles
Dan = Daniel
Deut = Deuteronomy

Esth = Esther
Exod = Exodus
Ezek = Ezekiel
Ezra = Ezra
Gen = Genesis
Hab = Habakkuk
Hag = Haggai
Hos = Hosea
Isa = Isaiah
Jer = Jeremiah
Job = Job
Jonah = Jonah
Josh = Joshua
Judg = Judges
1 Kgs = First Book of Kings
2 Kgs = Second Book of Kings
Mal = Malachi
Mic = Micah
Nah = Nahum
Neh = Nehemiah
Num = Numbers
Obad = Obadiah
Prov = Proverbs
Ps(s) = Psalm(s)
1 Sam = First Book of Samuel
2 Sam = Second Book of Samuel
Zech = Zechariah
Zeph = Zephaniah

**OT (A) = Old Testament (Apocrypha)**

Add Esth = Additions to Esther
1 Macc = First Book of Maccabees
Sg Three = Prayer of Azariah (Song of Three Jews)
Sir = Sirach (Ecclesiasticus)
Tob = Tobit

**Punctuation Usage**

/ = indicates where one line of poetic text ends and another begins

(biblical notation) = see the specific biblical verse(s) in parentheses for more information

– = range of verses following a colon (8:3–4)

— = range of verses from a verse in one chapter to a verse in another chapter (8:3—9:4)

a, b, c = designates first (a), second (b), third (c), etc. sentence in a verse of Scripture or a line of poetic text

Q = Quelle, a source shared by the authors of Matthew's Gospel and Luke's Gospel

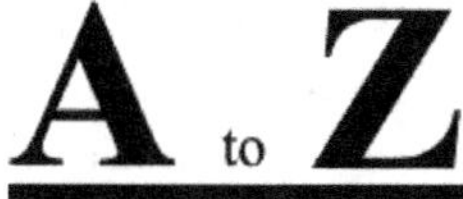


# Introduction

## TITLE

### Biblical Prophets

Most Bible readers know that there is a section of the Scriptures devoted to prophets, usually divided into major and minor. The major prophets are those who have the longest books: Isaiah, Jeremiah, Lamentations, Ezekiel, and Daniel. The minor prophets are those who have short books: Hosea, Joel, Amos, Obadiah, Jonah, Micah, Nahum, Habakkuk, Zephaniah, Haggai, Zechariah, Malachi. That brings the total of prophets to seventeen. But what about the biblical prophets who have no book named after them?

The prophets Elijah and Elisha, both of whom have no book named after them, are found in the HB (OT) First and Second Book of Kings, in which their prophecies and deeds are embedded in over ten chapters of text. However, there are over eighty more prophets and prophetesses, whose deeds and words are found narrated in other biblical books. In some cases only a name is mentioned, and in other cases a chapter may be devoted to them. In total, 104 entries for prophets and prophetesses can be found within biblical literature.

The people of Israel and the Jesus movement that evolved from them are conspicuous for their prophets. While most prophets were distinguished by their garments and diets, many are remembered for only a few words. The word prophet means to *bubble forth* words, like a fountain bubbles water. Biblical prophets and prophetesses experienced the LORD (God) communicating to them, and then they shared what they heard in prophecy with others. In other words, God entrusted them with some truth that he wanted to make known.

In biblical literature, prophets and prophetesses are sometimes named seer, one who sees with an inner eye, what today we might call deep insight. Seers are often given visions by the Divine. Those whose visions, words, and prophecies came true are known as true prophets, whereas those whose visions, words, and prophecies did not come true are known as false prophets. No matter if a man or woman is labeled a true or false prophet or prophetess, he or she can be found in biblical literature.

Ancient people considered prophets and prophetesses to have received a personal communication directly from God: "Thus says the LORD." The communication had to be delivered faithfully. This meant that prophets and prophetesses were mediators between the LORD (God) and people. Some prophets and prophetesses delivered truth that was difficult for the recipients to hear. Other prophets and prophetesses predicted events to happen; based on then-current perspectives, logical conclusions could be reached with divine assistance. For example, watching the Assyrian army conquer kingdom after kingdom would lead to the conclusion that Israel was next, or watching the Babylonian army conquer kingdom after kingdom would lead to the conclusion that Judah was next. Thus, a prophet's or prophetess' prediction is less about telling the future and more about telling the consequences of what will happen, if what is happening continues to happen into the future. Thus, prophets and prophetesses are messengers from God; they were sent by the LORD to speak to people.

## From A to Z

In the entries that follow, there are 104 prophets and prophetesses presented in seven chapters in alphabetical order. Each entry begins with the prophet's or prophetess' name, and is followed by a Scripture text illustrating some aspect of the named prophet or prophetess, a reflection highlighting the prophet or prophetess, a Meditation/Journal question for further reflection by the reader, and a Psalm Response consisting of a few verses of a psalm that illustrate the prophet's or prophetess' life or message.

While the prophets are arranged from A to Z, there are some letters in the alphabet that do not have the name of a prophet that begins with that letter. Thus, for Q, R, T, W, X, and Y something about the activity of prophets is explored. For example, since no prophet's name begins with Q, the function of quake—as in earthquake—is examined as an element in a prophetic theophany. Since no prophet's name begins with R, the function of the town named Ramah is examined, as it appears in biblical prophecy.

## Known & Unknown

As already noted above, many prophets and prophetesses are well known. But there are others who are unknown. And there are some who are identified otherwise, but qualify as a prophet or prophetess. For example, modern biblical scholarship has identified three different prophets Isaiah; each is given his due below, including Isaiah's wife, who is presented as a prophetess in Isaiah 1.

## Notes on the Bible

### *Three Parts*

The Bible is divided into two parts: The Hebrew Bible (Old Testament) and the Christian Bible (New Testament). The Hebrew Bible consists of thirty-nine named books accepted by Jews and Protestants as Holy Scripture. The Old Testament also contains those thirty-nine books plus seven to fifteen more named books or parts of books called the Apocrypha or the Deuterocanonical Books; the Old Testament is accepted by Catholics and several other Christian denominations as Holy Scripture. The Christian Bible, consisting of twenty-seven named books, is also called the New Testament; it is accepted by Christians as Holy Scripture. Thus, in this work:

—**Hebrew Bible (Old Testament)**, abbreviated **HB (OT)**, indicates that a book is found both in the Hebrew Bible and the Old Testament;

—**Old Testament (Apocrypha)**, abbreviated **OT (A)**, indicates that a book is found only in the Old Testament Apocrypha and not in the Hebrew Bible;

—and **Christian Bible (New Testament)**, abbreviated **CB (NT)**, indicates that a book is found only in the Christian Bible or New Testament.

In notating biblical texts, the first number refers to the chapter in the book, and the second number (following the colon) refers to the verse within the chapter. Thus, HB (OT) Isa 7:11 means that the quotation comes from Isaiah, chapter 7, verse 11. OT (A) Sir 39:30 means that the quotation comes from Sirach, chapter 39, verse 30. CB (NT) Mark 6:2 means that the quotation comes from Mark's Gospel, chapter 6, verse 2. When more than one sentence appears in a verse, the letters a, b, c, etc. indicate the sentence being referenced in the verse. Thus, HB (OT) 2 Kgs 1:6a means that the quotation comes from the Second Book of Kings, chapter 1, verse 6, sentence 1. Also, poetry, such as the Psalms and sections of Judith, Proverbs, Isaiah, and others may be noted using the letters a, b, c, etc. to indicate the lines being used. Thus, Ps 16:4a refers to the first line of verse 4 of Psalm 16; there are two more lines of verse 4: b and c.

Because there may be a difference in the verse numbers between the *New Revised Standard Version Updated Edition* (NRSVue) and the Vulgate (the Latin translation of the Septuagint, such as *The New American Bible Revised Edition* [NABRE]), verse numbers may be off by a verse or two. This is true particularly with the Psalms, but with other books as well. Thus, NRSVue Isaiah 9:2–7 is NABRE (Vulgate) Isaiah 9:1–6; NRSVue Isaiah 9:2–4, 6–7 is NABRE (Vulgate) Isaiah 9:1–3, 5–6. Introductory material to Bibles usually indicates which verse-numbering is being used.

In the HB (OT) and the OT (A), the reader often sees LORD (note all capital letters). Because God's name (Yahweh or YHWH, referred to as the Tetragrammaton) is not to be pronounced, the name Adonai (meaning *Lord*) is substituted for Yahweh when a biblical text is read. When a biblical text is translated and printed, LORD (Gen 2:4) is used to alert the reader to what the text actually states: Yahweh. Furthermore, when the biblical author writes Lord Yahweh, printers present Lord GOD (note all capital letters for GOD; Gen 15:2) to avoid the printed ambiguity of LORD LORD. The Psalms in *The Message* substitute GOD (note all capital letters) for Yahweh. When the reference is to Jesus, the word printed is Lord (note capital L and lower-case letters); Luke 11:1). When writing about a lord (note all lower-case letters; Matt 18:25) with servants, no capital L is used.

In this book, *cf* (meaning *confer*) has not been used. Biblical notations placed in parentheses indicate where the reference can be found in the Bible. For example, the Second Book of Samuel records King David writing a song (2 Sam 22:1–51). The notation in parentheses is given to the reader, who may wish to look up the full reference in his or her Bible. In some instances, a few notations appear in parentheses; again, the reader may wish to see the references in their contexts.

## Bibles

Most Bible readers are not aware that there is no such thing as the original Bible! The fact is: There are Bibles. First, there is the Jewish Bible, often called the Hebrew Bible; its books were collected and completed between 70 and 90 CE based on the Jerusalem canon (collection) in this order: Torah (Genesis, Exodus, Leviticus, Numbers, Deuteronomy), Prophets (Isaiah, Jeremiah,

Ezekiel, etc.), and Writings (Job, Psalms, Proverbs, etc.). It is important to note the arrangement of the collected books. Second, there is—for want of a better name—the Christian Hebrew Bible, completed in the fourth century CE, but not defined until after the Reformation. It consists of Torah, Writings, and Prophets. It is important to note the (re)ordering of the collected books. Christianity took the Jewish (Hebrew) Bible and rearranged the order of its books! Then, Christianity named it the Old Testament.

The Jerusalem canon, obviously, is the collection of biblical books used in Jerusalem and its environs. A large community of Jews, however, lived in Alexandria, Egypt. To the Jerusalem canon (books in Hebrew and Aramaic) they added books in Greek, the language they spoke; this collection is the Alexandrine canon. They also translated the Jerusalem canon's books from Hebrew and Aramaic into Greek. That translation, containing books and parts of books not in the Jerusalem canon, is called the Septuagint (abbreviated LXX). Later, the Septuagint was translated into Latin; it is known as the Vulgate. Every time a book of the Bible is translated, it picks up something and it loses something; that is because there is no such thing as literary equivalence.

Thus, we have (1) the Hebrew Bible—the Jewish Bible, (2) the Hebrew Bible (Old Testament)—the rearranged books of the Hebrew Bible, and (3) the Christian Bible—twenty-seven books originally written in Greek. The Protestant Bible contains only the books in the Jerusalem canon, but rearranged into the Old Testament, plus the Christian Bible books; the Catholic Bible contains the books in the Alexandrine collection plus the Christian Bible books.

The extra books or parts of books found in the Catholic Bible (and coming from the Alexandrine collection of the Jewish Bible), but not found in a Protestant Bible, are collectively referred to as the Apocrypha or Deuterocanonical Books. They include Tobit, Judith, additions to Esther, Wisdom (of Solomon), Sirach (Ecclesiasticus), Baruch, Letter of Jeremiah, Prayer of Azariah (addition to Daniel), Susanna (addition to Daniel), Bel and the Dragon (addition to Daniel), 1 Maccabees, 2 Maccabees, 1 Esdras, Prayer of Manasseh, Psalm 151, 3 Maccabees, 2 Esdras, and 4 Maccabees. Not every Christian group, such as Catholics, accepts all the books in the Apocrypha as Scripture; for example, out of the four books of Maccabees, Catholics accept only 1 and 2 Maccabees. In Catholic Bibles, the additional books are placed with similar books. Thus, First and Second Maccabees are inserted with the historical books; the books of Wisdom and Sirach are found in the wisdom literature section.

Thus, there is no single or original Bible; there are many Bibles; it depends on what books a specific denomination or group (Jews, Christians) accepts as Scripture. The Bible that contains any book that any group accepts as Scripture is *The Access Bible* (updated edition): *New Revised Standard Version with the*

*Apocrypha*, general editors Gail R. O'Day and David Petersen, published in New York by Oxford University Press in 1999 and updated in 2011. In 2021, the NRSV was published by Zondervan as the New Revised Standard Version updated edition (NRSVue), which, like its predecessor, contains all the books any group of people may consider to be a part of their Bible.

Thus, a Bible reader should keep in mind the following: In a Christian Bible, The Old Testament consists of the rearranged books found in the Hebrew (Jewish) Bible. Roman Catholics and some others add some books and parts of books to that Old Testament because they were found in the Alexandrine collection. In general, Protestants do not add books to the Old Testament; they follow the Jerusalem collection of books, but rearrange them as noted above. Almost all Christians accept the twenty-seven books of the New Testament; there are a few groups who reject one or another of the books in the collection.

Thus, as you can see, this can become difficult to navigate, especially when someone says, "The Bible says . . . ." The astute Bible reader needs to ask, "Which book in which Bible says that?" There is no such thing as the original Bible. There are Bibles, various libraries of books collected over three thousand years by individuals and groups who declared their collection (canon) to be Scripture. When engaged in Bible study, it is also important to note that the Bible is a library of books written by different authors at different times in history; it is not a single book. While the authors of various books often agree with each other, there are occasions when they disagree with each other.

## Presuppositions

The HB (OT) begins as stories passed on by word of mouth from one person to another. Sometime during the oral transmission stage, authors decided to collect the oral stories and write them. A change occurs immediately. One does not tell a story the same way one writes a story. Repetition and correction occur in oral story-telling. Except for future emendations by copyists, single statements by characters and plot structure dominate written stories. Furthermore, in both oral and written story-telling, types or models are employed. In the HB (OT), for example, Joshua and Elijah are types of Moses. In the CB (NT) Elizabeth becomes a type of Hannah, who is herself a type of Sarah. When orally narrating or writing a story, the teller or author consciously creates one character as a type of another to make the character and his or her words and actions intelligible to the hearer or reader.

In the CB (NT) the oldest gospel is Mark's account of Jesus' victory. The author of Matthew's Gospel copied and shortened about eighty percent of

Mark's material into his book and then added other stories to make the work longer. The author of Luke's Gospel copied and shortened about fifty percent of Mark's material into his orderly account and then added other stories to make the work much longer. The material shared by Matthew and Luke is called Q—from the German word *Quelle*, meaning *Source*—by biblical scholars. Mark's Gospel begins as oral story-telling, lasting for about forty years in that form. An unidentified author, called Mark for the sake of convenience, collects the oral stories, sets a plot, and writes the first gospel around 70 CE. Because Jesus was expected to return soon, no one had thought about recording what he had said and done until Mark came along and realized that he was not returning as quickly as had been thought. About ten years after Mark finished his gospel, Matthew needed to adopt Mark's narrative—originally intended for a peasant gentile readership—to a Jewish audience. And about twenty years after Mark finished his gospel, Luke needed to adapt Mark's poor gentile-intended work for a rich, upper class, urban, gentile readership. The author of John's Gospel did not know the existence of the other three works collectively named synoptic gospels. A point often overlooked by modern readers is the fact that they are not the intended readers of biblical texts. Every biblical book was written to a specific group of people at a specific time in history. Thus, Paul did not write to people living in the United States; he wrote in Greek to people living in Rome, Corinth, and Thessalonica. Modern readers are reading an English translation (and interpretation) with Roman-Greco cultural presuppositions underlying the text.

Furthermore, letters and gospels were not first intended to be read privately as is done today. They were meant to be heard in a group. The very low rate of literacy in the first century would have never dictated many copies of texts since most people could not read, and their standard practice was to listen to another read the letters and stories to them. Thus, what began as oral story-telling passed on by word of mouth became written story-telling preserved in gospels. A careful reading of Mark's Gospel will reveal the orality still embedded in the text, especially evident in the repetition of words and the organization of stories in three parts. In rewriting Mark, Matthew and Luke removed the last traces of oral story-telling.

The letters of Paul are older than the gospels. Biblical scholars divide the letters of Paul into the authentic letters—those written by Paul (Romans, Galatians, Philippians, etc.)—and those written by someone else in Paul's name—second generation Pauline letters (Ephesians, Colossians, Titus, etc.). The latter group of letters usually develop Pauline thought for a new generation of Christians. The reader of letters needs to keep in mind that the letter was not addressed to him or her; it was addressed to a specific group of believers in the mid- to late-first century CE. In addition to the Pauline body of letters, there are other letters that were gathered and placed in the CB (NT) canon (collection), such as James, 1 and 2 Peter, Jude, etc. These anonymous letters were written in the name of an apostle to give them authority in the Christian communities to which they were addressed.

Furthermore, it is important to understand that there are three different Pauls presented in the CB (NT). There is the Acts of the Apostles Paul, who is presented by the same author who wrote Luke's Gospel; in other words, Luke-Acts is a two-volume work. There is original Paul, the man who wrote or dictated letters attributed to him. And there is second-generation Paul, others who wrote under Paul's name to update some of original Paul's ideas for the next generation of believers. The caution here is to be sure that a reader is not interpreting original Paul through the lens of the Acts of the Apostles Paul. While all three Pauls are similar, their theological positions are quite different.

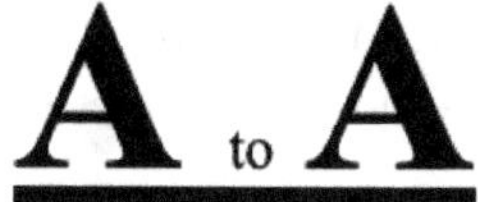

# 1

# A

## FROM AARON TO AZARIAH

### Aaron

**Scripture**: "The LORD said to Moses, '. . . [Y]our brother Aaron shall be your prophet. You shall speak all that I command you, and your brother Aaron shall tell Pharaoh to let the Israelites go out of his land.'" (Exod 7:1–2, NRSVue)

**Reflection**: As the first high priest of the Israelites, Aaron, meaning *exalted* or *high mountain*, is Moses' brother; they have a sister named Miriam. Designated as a prophet by the LORD because he could speak well (Exod 4:14), Aaron and his sons are consecrated as priests to serve the LORD (Exod 28:1–5). There are a variety of scriptural traditions concerning Aaron woven throughout the HB (OT) books of Exodus, Leviticus, Numbers, and Deuteronomy; often, the various traditions do not agree with each other. For example, according to Numbers, Aaron is buried on Mount Hor (Num 20:22–29), but according to Deuteronomy, he is buried at Moserah (Deut 10:6). Through the ages of both oral and written story-telling, the historical Aaron has been obscured and transfigured. In the CB (NT), the unique Letter to the Hebrews states that Aaron was called by God (Heb 5:4), even though the Levitical priesthood was imperfect, according to Hebrews (7:11). The relationship between the brothers Moses and Aaron is similar to the relationship between God and Moses. Aaron is Moses' prophet or spokesperson, just like Moses is God's prophet or messenger.

**Meditation/Journal**: In your life is there a spokesperson, messenger, or prophet? If so, who is it? If not, whom do you consider to fill the roles of spokesperson, messenger, or prophet?

**Psalm Response**: "Honor GOD, our God; worship his rule! / Holy. Yes holy. / Moses and Aaron were his priests . . . . / He spoke from the pillar of cloud. / And they did what he said; they kept the law he gave them. / And then GOD, our God, answered them . . . . / Lift high, GOD our God; worship at his holy mountain. / Holy. Yes, holy is GOD our God. (Ps 99:5, 7–9, TM)

## Abel

**Scripture**: Jesus said to the lawyers: "Woe . . . to you experts in the law! For you load people with burdens hard to bear, and you yourselves do not lift a finger to ease them. Woe to you! For you build the tombs of the prophets whom your ancestors killed. So you are witnesses and approve of the deeds of your ancestors, for they killed them, and you build their tombs. For this reason the Wisdom of God, said, 'I will send them prophets and apostles, some of whom they will kill and persecute,' so that this generation may be charged with the blood of all the prophets shed since the foundation of the world, from the blood of Abel to the blood of Zechariah . . . .'" (Luke 11:46–51, NRSVue)

**Reflection**: Abel, whose name means *son*, was the second son of Adam and Eve in the HB (OT) book of Genesis. He was a shepherd, whose sacrifice was acceptable to God and who was killed by his brother Cain (Gen 4:1–16). While he is not named a prophet in the HB (OT), he is associated with prophets by Q in the CB (NT). Q, from the German *Quelle*, meaning *source*, is a collection of Jesus' sayings imbedded in Matthew's Gospel and in Luke's Gospel. The Matthean version of the above Scripture passage can be found at 23:29–35. The Lukan Jesus indicts lawyers for building tombs for the prophets, who were slain by their ancestors. For the Lukan Jesus, this implies approval of their ancestors' deeds. While the Wisdom of God speaks in the HB (OT) book of Proverbs (1:20–33; 8:1–36), the saying about God sending prophets and apostles, who would be killed and persecuted, is not found in the Bible. The point of the above passage is that the intended Lukan readers (upper class gentiles) will associate Jewish lawyers, who reject Jesus and his apostles, as continuing to form a line with previous rejections. In other words, a line of prophetic rejection stretches from Abel through Zechariah to Jesus and his followers.

**Meditation/Journal**: In your family, what characteristic stretches from one of your ancestors to you? Explain.

**Psalm Response**: "The stone the masons discarded as flawed / is now the capstone! / This is GOD's work. / We rub our eyes—we can hardly believe it! / This is the very day GOD acted— / let's celebrate and be festive! / Salvation now, GOD. Salvation now! / Oh yes, GOD—a free and full life." (Ps 118:22–25, TM)

## Abram/Abraham

**Scripture**: ". . . God came to Abimelech in a dream by night and said to him, . . . '. . . [R]eturn the man's wife, for he is a prophet, and he will pray for you, and you shall live.'" (Gen 20:3, 7a, NRSVue)

**Reflection**: Abraham and his wife, Sarah, journeyed to Gerar, where he told King Abimelech that Sarah was his sister, as he had previously told Pharaoh in Egypt (Gen 12:10–20). If he had said that Sarah was his wife, the king or Pharoah could have killed him and taken Sarah as his wife. The LORD afflicts Pharaoh with great plagues—a foretaste of those in Exodus—but he appears in a dream to Abimelech, telling the king that Sarah is Abraham's wife, and he needs to return her to him; the LORD assures Abimelech that Abraham, being a prophet—the only time Abraham is identified as such in biblical literature—will pray for him. Indeed, after Abimelech restores Sarah to Abraham, the patriarch prays to God, who heals Abimelech, his wife, and his female slaves, so they can bear children (Gen 20:17–18). First, Abraham endangers Sarah's life to save his own! Second, all people are God's people, even Abimelech, a Canaanite king of Gerar. Third, not only is this sister-wife story about Abraham and Sarah duplicated in Genesis, but the sister-wife theme will appear again with Isaac and Rebekah in Gerar (Gen 26:6–11).

**Meditation/Journal**: When have you placed another person in some kind of jeopardy by lying about them or about yourself? Explain.

**Psalm Response**: "He's GOD, our God, / in charge of the whole earth. / And he remembers, remembers his Covenant— / for a thousand generations he's been as good as his word. / It's the Covenant he made with Abraham, / the same oath he swore to Isaac . . . . / Wandering from country to country, / drifting from pillar to post, / He permitted no one to abuse them. / He told kings to keep their hands off: / 'Don't you dare lay a hand on my anointed, / don't hurt a hair on the heads of my prophets.'" (Ps 105:7–9, 13–15, TM)

## Agabus

**Scripture**: "While we were staying [with Philip the evangelist and his four unmarried daughters, who had the gift of prophecy] for several days, a prophet named Agabus came down from Judea. He came to us and took Paul's belt, bound his own feet and hands with it, and said, 'Thus says the Holy Spirit, "This is the way the Jews in Jerusalem will bind the man who owns this belt and will hand him over to the gentiles."' When we heard this, we and the people there urged him not to go up to Jerusalem." (Acts 21:10–12, NRSVue)

**Reflection**: The reader of the CB (NT) book of the Acts of the Apostles was introduced to the prophet Agabus earlier in the work: ". . . [P]rophets came down from Jerusalem to Antioch. One of them named Agabus stood up and predicted by the Spirit that there would be a severe famine over all the world, and this took place during the reign of Claudius" (Acts 11:27–28, NRSVue) (41–54 CE). Historically, while there was a famine during Claudius' reign, the character Agabus seems to appear and disappear as needed by the author of the CB (NT) Acts of the Apostles. He makes this clear when he states that Agabus predicted the severe famine by the Spirit; by the fact that the famine occurred confirms that he is a prophet. Similarly, Agabus engages in prophetic enactment using Paul's belt and prophesizing again in the Holy Spirit to indicate what will happen to Paul in the future, if he travels to Jerusalem. This propels the reader forward to keep reading to find out what does happen to Paul in the narrative. Spoiler alert: Agabus' prediction comes true, of course. He is a trustworthy prophet.

**Meditation/Journal**: In your life, what unknown prophet has indicated something about you that did occur afterward?

**Psalm Response**: May GOD "Give you what your heart desires, / Accomplish your plans. / When you win, we plan to raise the roof / and lead the parade with our banners. / May all your wishes come true! / That cinches it—help's coming, / an answer's on the way, / everything's going to work out." (Ps 20:4–6, TM)

## Agur

**Scripture**: "The words of Agur . . . . An oracle. . . . / I have not learned wisdom, / nor have I knowledge of the holy ones. / Who has ascended to heaven and come down? / Who has gathered the wind in the hollow of the hand? / Who has wrapped the waters in a garment? / Who has established all the ends of the earth? / What is the person's name? (Prov 30:1, 3–4, NRSVue)

**Reflection**: Agur, who appears but one time in the Bible, is considered a prophet because he gives an oracle (which did not come from his own efforts), which was copied into the end of the HB (OT) book of Proverbs. Upon careful analysis, it looks like Agur has borrowed extensively from other biblical books. For instance, the series of questions beginning with *Who?* echo Moses' words in the HB (OT) book of Deuteronomy: "Who will go up to heaven for us and get [the commandment] for us so that we may hear it and observe it?" (Deut 30:12, NRSVue) and "Who will cross to the other side of the sea for us and get [the commandment] for us so that we may hear it and observe it?" (Deut 30:13, NRSVue) Furthermore, the verses echo the divine questions beginning with *Who?* in Job 38:1–41:34 and scattered through Isaiah 40:12–45:19.

**Meditation/Journal**: What is the name of the person who came from heaven and then ascended to heaven, who gathered the wind into the hollow of his hand, who wrapped the waters in a garment, who established all the ends of the earth? Explain.

**Psalm Response**: "When I was beleaguered and bitter, / totally consumed by envy, / I was totally ignorant, a dumb ox / in your very presence. / I'm still in your presence, / but you've taken my hand. / You wisely and tenderly lead me, / and then you bless me. / You're all I want in heaven! / You're all I want on earth! / . . . I'm in the very presence of God— / oh, how refreshing it is! / I've made Lord GOD my home. / God, I'm telling the world what you do!" (Ps 73:21–25, 28, TM)

## Ahab

**Scripture**: "Thus says the LORD of hosts: [A]ll of you exiles whom I sent away from Jerusalem to Babylon, hear the word of the LORD: Thus says the LORD of hosts, the God of Israel, concerning Ahab . . . , who [is] prophesying a lie to you in my name . . . . And on account of them this curse shall be used by all the exiles from Judah in Babylon: 'The LORD make you like . . . Ahab, whom the king of Babylon roasted in the fire,' because [he has] perpetrated outrage in Israel and . . . [has] spoken in my name lying words that I did not command [him]; I am the one who knows and bears witness, says the LORD." (Jer 29:17, 19–23, NRSVue)

**Reflection**: The prophet Ahab is not the same as King Ahab of Israel. According to the HB (OT) prophet Jeremiah, the prophet Ahab is false. Jeremiah does not record what his false prophesy is, but he does note that Nebuchadnezzar, King of Babylon, roasted him in fire, at the LORD's instigation (Jer 29:21). This is meant to fulfill the LORD's words to Moses spoken in the HB (OT) book of

Deuteronomy: ". . . [A]ny prophet who presumes to speak in my name a word that I have not commanded the prophet to speak or who speaks in the name of other gods, that prophet shall die" (Deut 18:20, NRSVue). A prophet is declared false if what he says does not take place. The prophet Jeremiah urged the exiles to build houses, plant gardens, marry, conceive children, and seek the welfare of the city in which they were exiled through prayer (Jer 29:4–7). More specifically, he urged the exiles to beware of false prophets, whom the LORD did not send (Jer 29:8–9). It is only after the time of the exile was complete that the LORD would bring back the exiles to Jerusalem (Jer 29:10–14). While it is conjecture, Ahab must have been disputing or contradicting the LORD's words spoken by the prophet Jeremiah.

**Meditation/Journal**: Whom have you recently identified as a false prophet? Explain.

**Psalm Response**: "You're blessed when you stay on course, / walking steadily on the road revealed by GOD. / You're blessed when you follow his directions, / doing your best to find him. / That's right—you don't go off on your own; / you walk straight along the road he set. / You, GOD, prescribed the right way to live; / now you expect us to live it. / Oh, that my steps might be steady, / keeping to the course you set; / Then I'd never have any regrets / in comparing my life with your counsel." (Ps 119:1–6, TM)

## Ahijah

**Scripture**: ". . . [W]hen Jeroboam was leaving Jerusalem, the prophet Ahijah . . . found him on the road. Ahijah had clothed himself with a new garment. The two of them were alone in the open country when Ahijah laid hold of the new garment he was wearing and tore it into twelve pieces. He then said to Jeroboam, 'Take for yourself ten pieces, for thus says the LORD, the God of Israel: See, I am about to tear the kingdom from the hand of Solomon and will give you ten tribes.'" (1 Kgs 11:29–31, NRSVue)

**Reflection**: The prophet Ahijah makes his first biblical appearance in 1 Kings 11:29, announcing to Jeroboam I that he would lead the rebellion against King Solomon of Judah's successor—Rehoboam—and form a confederation of the ten northern tribes of Israel called the Kingdom of Israel with him as its first king. The act of Ahijah tearing his new garment into twelve pieces and giving ten of the pieces to Jeroboam is called an enacted prophecy by biblical scholars. In other words, the prophet Ahijah enacts what will take place shortly in the future. Ahijah is a prophet at Shiloh (1 Kgs 14:2) to whom Jeroboam sends his wife when his son, Abijah, falls ill. Ahijah does not have comforting words to deliver to Jeroboam's wife about Abijah. Nevertheless, as God's faithful prophet, he delivers the word of the LORD that was given him (1 Kgs 14:6–17). The last biblical appearance of Abijah identifies him as the LORD's servant (1 Kgs 14:18).

**Meditation/Journal**: In your life, who has been like the prophet Ahijah, announcing words difficult to hear?

**Psalm Response**: "How well God must like you— / . . . [Y]ou thrill to GOD's Word, / you chew on Scripture day and night. / You're like a tree replanted in Eden, / bearing fresh fruit every month, / Never dropping a leaf, / always in blossom. / You're not at all like the wicked, / who are mere windblown dust— / GOD charts the road you take . . . . (Ps 1:1a, 2–4, 6a, TM)

## Amos

**Scripture**: Amaziah [, the priest of Bethel,] said to Amos, 'O seer, go; flee away to the land of Judah, earn your bread there, and prophesy there, but never again prophesy at Bethel, for it is the king's sanctuary, and it is a temple of the kingdom.' Then Amos answered Amaziah, 'I am no prophet nor a prophet's son, but I am a herdsman and a dresser of sycamore trees, and the LORD took me from following the flock, and the LORD said to me, "Go, prophesy to my people Israel."'" (Amos 7:12–15, NRSVue)

**Reflection**: Amaziah is a priest of Bethel, a shrine established by Jeroboam I (931–910 BCE), when he became the first king of Israel; one of Jeroboam's descendants—Jeroboam II (782–753 BCE)—sits on Israel's throne. Amos, a herdsman and dresser of sycamore trees, is from the southern Kingdom of Judah. Amaziah tells Amos to go home and preach in Judah. Amos responds that he is not a professional prophet; he does not earn his living prophesying. He brings an unexpected but genuine divine revelation to the Northern Kingdom of Israel. His message is "Israel must go into exile away from his land" (Amos 7:11, NRSVue). Amos' words came true in 722 BCE, when Assyria captured Samaria, the capital of Israel. The record of his encounter with Amaziah is the only narrative about Amos' career; the rest of the nine-chapter book contains words about social justice. Amos announces Israel's social justice violations and divine judgment and punishment for the lack of political, judicial, economic, and abuse-of-power justice. At the time of Amos, the Northern Kingdom of Israel was enjoying a period of abundant prosperity, but the poor were being used and trampled by those making a lot of money!

**Meditation/Journal**: In your life, where do you find a lack of political, judicial, economic, and power justice?

**Psalm Response**: "GOD, you smiled on your good earth! / Love and Truth meet in the street, / Right Living and Whole Living embrace and kiss! / Truth sprouts green from the ground, / Right Living pours down from the skies! / Oh yes! GOD gives Goodness and Beauty; / our land responds with Bounty and Blessing. / Right Living strides out before him, / and clears a path for his passage." (Ps 85:1a, 10–13, TM)

## Anna

**Scripture**: "There was also a prophet[ess], Anna the daughter of Phanuel, of the tribe of Asher. She was of a great age, having lived with her husband seven years after her marriage, then as a widow to the age of eighty-four. She never left the temple but worshiped there with fasting and prayer night and day. At that moment she came and began to praise God and to speak about the child to all who were looking for the redemption of Jerusalem." (Luke 2:36–38, NRSVue)

**Reflection**: Anna, the Greek form of the Hebrew Hannah, is a prophetess, who recognized the infant Jesus as the Messiah, and whose biblical appearance is unique to Luke's Gospel. Anna makes a single appearance when Jesus' parents bring him to Jerusalem to present him in the temple. The author of the CB (NT) gospel according to Luke displays two of his favorite motifs in narrating the story. First, Anna, a female prophet, serves as a balance to the majority of the story centered on Simeon, a male prophet (Luke 2:22–35). Throughout the gospel and the author's second volume—Acts of the Apostles—he pairs female characters with male characters. Second, while the practice of living in the temple is legend, the prophetess' practice of fasting and prayer day and night are classic expressions of prophetic piety. Together, Anna and Simeon represent the people of God first welcoming the prophet Jesus in contrast to the usual biblical first rejection of prophets sent by God to his people.

**Meditation/Journal**: Identify someone you consider a modern-day prophet(ess). What is his or her message? How is that message generally received? Explain.

**Canticle Response**: "God, you can now release your servant; / release me in peace as you promised. / With my own eyes I've seen your salvation; / it's now out in the open for everyone to see: / A God-revealing light to the non-Jewish nations, / and of glory for your people Israel." (Luke 2:29–32, TM)

## Antichrist

**Scripture**: "As you have heard that antichrist is coming, so now many antichrists have come. They went out from us, but they did not belong to us, for if they had belonged to us they would have remained with us. But by going out they made it plain that none of them belongs to us." (1 John 2:18b, 19, NRSVue)

**Reflection**: The author of the CB (NT) First Letter of John warns his readers about antichrists, those who deny that Jesus is God's anointed (Christ) (1 John 2:22), In so doing, the antichrist is "one who denies the Father and the Son" (1 John 2:22, NRSVue), because "[n]o one who denies the Son has the Father" but "everyone who confesses the Son has the Father also" (1 John 2:23, NRSVue). The author identifies antichrists as "false prophets [who] have gone out into the world" (1 John 4:1, NRSVue); those false prophets were at one time members of the community of believers. "[E]very spirit that confesses that Jesus Christ has come in the flesh is from God, and every spirit that does not confess Jesus is not from God. And this is the spirit of the antichrist, of which you have heard . . . it is already in the world" (1 John 4:3, NRSVue). The author names as antichrists—false prophets—those who emerge from his community of believers as opponents, namely, those who deny that Jesus is God's anointed. According to the author, the truth—the correct confession—is that the human Jesus was also the divine Christ.

**Meditation/Journal**: Whom do you identify as an antichrist, one who left a community (church, neighborhood, volunteer organization, book club, etc.) to which you belonged and became an opponent of the community?

**Psalm Response**: "I love you, GOD— / you make me strong. / GOD is bedrock under my feet, / the castle in which I live, / my rescuing knight. / My God—the high crag / where I run for dear life, / hiding behind the boulders, / safe in the granite hideout. / . . . [M]e he caught—reached all the way / from sky to sea; he pulled me out / Of that ocean of hate, that enemy chaos, / the void in which I was drowning. / . . . GOD stuck by me. / He stood me up on a wide-open field; / I stood there saved—surprised to be loved!" (Ps 18:1–2, 16–17, 19, TM)

## Asaph

**Scripture**: "King Hezekiah [of Judah (716–687 BCE)] and the officials commanded the Levites to sing praises to the LORD with the words of David and of the seer Asaph. They sang praises with gladness, and they bowed down and worshiped." (2 Chr 29:30)

**Reflection**: While there are at least five other biblical men bearing the name Asaph, it is only in the Second Book of Chronicles that a specific Asaph is identified as a seer or prophet. He was appointed by David over the service of song and by Solomon in Temple services (1Chr 6:39; 15:17). Asaph is identified as a singer (1 Chr 15:19), and his name appears in titles of Psalms 50 and 73–83; the name not only indicates that Asaph may have composed the psalms, but that the collection of psalms belonged to a Levitical guild of singers (Ezra 2:41; Neh 7:44), who considered themselves descendants of Asaph. King Hezekiah instituted religious reform in Jerusalem by cleansing the Temple, restoring Passover, and making other reforms of the Temple cult. The author of the Second Book of Chronicles notes that he "did what was right in the sight of the LORD" (2 Chr 29:2, NRSVue), a description not used frequently! The chronicler notes in the Scripture passage above that during Hezekiah's reign, there was a group of singers who sang psalms and traced their origin to Asaph the prophet.

**Meditation/Journal**: What do you consider one of your special talents to be? Which of your ancestors do you consider to be the origin of that talent?

**Psalm Response**: An Asaph Psalm: "Listen, dear friends, to God's truth, / bend your ears to what I tell you. / I'm chewing on the morsel of a proverb; / I'll let you in on the sweet old truths, / Stories we heard from our fathers, / counsel we learned at our mother's knee. / We're not keeping this to ourselves, / we're passing it along to the next generation— / GOD's fame and fortune, / the marvelous things he has done." (Ps 78:1–4, TM)

## Azariah

**Scripture**: "The spirit of God came upon Azariah son of Oded. He went out to meet [King] Asa [of Judah (911–870 BCE)] and said to him, 'Hear me, Asa . . . : The LORD is with you while you are with him. If you seek him, he will be found by you, but if you abandon him, he will abandon you." (2 Chr 15:1–2, NRSVue)

**Reflection**: According to the chronicler, King "Asa did what was good and right in the sight of the LORD his God" (2 Chr 14:2, NRSVue); he is one of only a few kings who are described as such! After inheriting David's throne from his father, King Abijah (913–911 BCE), he began a reform, which included removing idolatry from the land of Judah; he even removed his mother because she had made an idol (2 Chr 15:16)! He was encouraged to continue his reforms by the prophet Azariah; the chronicler states, "When Asa heard [Azariah's] words, the prophecy of Azariah son of Oded, he took courage and put away the abominable idols from all the land of Judah . . ." (2 Chr 15:8, NRSVue), even repairing the altar of the LORD that was in front of the Temple (2 Chr 15:9). In the Bible, Azariah is a popular name; there are at least twenty-eight men bearing that name in biblical books. Azariah, son of Oded, is the only prophet mentioned during King Asa's forty-one years on Judah's throne.

**Meditation/Journal**: During your life, what do you consider to be one wrong that you have righted? Explain.

**Psalm Response**: "Listen, GOD! Please, pay attention! / Can you make sense of these ramblings, / my groans and cries? / King-God, I need your help. / Every morning / you'll hear me at it again. / Every morning / I lay out the pieces of my life / on your altar / and watch for fire to descend. / I enter your house; here I am, / prostrate in your inner sanctum, / Waiting for directions . . . . (Ps 5:1–3, 7b–8a, TM)

# Biblical Prophets

# B to E

# 2

# B–E

## FROM BALAAM TO EZEKIEL

### Balaam

**Scripture**: ". . . Balak . . . was king of Moab . . . . He sent messengers to Balaam . . . to summon him, saying, 'A people has come out of Egypt; they have spread over the face of the earth, and they have settled next to me. Come now, curse this people for me . . . . I know that whomever you bless is blessed, and whomever you curse is cursed.'" (Num 22:4b–6, NRSVue)

**Reflection**: The complete story concerning Balaam is embedded in the HB (OT) book of Numbers (22:1—24:25). According to the narrator of the book, Balaam claims that "the LORD speaks to [him]" (Num 22:8–9, 12). At first, God tells Balaam not to go with Balak's messengers because he doesn't want cursed the people he has blessed (Num 22:12). Then, God tells him to go, but to say only what God tells him to say (Num 22:20). To further indicate that God is in charge of whatever Balaam says or does, an angel of the LORD stands in the road in Balaam's way (Num 22:23–35). With a note of humor, Balaam's donkey can see the angel of the LORD—a code phrase for God—but Balaam can't at first see him. After Balaam is met by Balak, Balaam tells him that he doesn't have the power to say just anything. "The word God puts in my mouth, that is what I must say" (Num 22:38). Then, begins a series of four oracles. In each, Balak instructs Balaam to curse the Israelites, and he ends up blessing them: "Must I not take care to say what the LORD puts into my mouth?" he asks Balak after the first oracle of blessing (Num 23:12). After the second oracle of blessing, he tells Balak, "Whatever the LORD says, that is what I must do" (Num 23:26). After the third oracle of blessing, Balak states, "I summoned you to curse my enemies, but instead you have blessed them these three times" (Num 24:10b). Balaam responds by telling him that he was not able to go beyond the word of the LORD (Num 24:13). Before he leaves Balak, Balaam utters a fourth oracle of blessing as "one who hears the words of God / and knows the knowledge of the Most High, / who sees the vision of the Almighty, / who falls down but with eyes uncovered" (Num 24:16). After sufficiently blessing the Israelites four times, Balaam leaves Balak and returns to his home. Because God spoke through Balaam, he is considered a prophet, even though in biblical literature he is named as one who practiced divination (Josh 13:22). Balaam is well-known in other biblical literature (Deut 23:4–5; 2 Pet 2:15; Jude 1:11; Rev 2:14). His death is recorded in Numbers 31:8. Thus, while Balaam is depicted as a diviner and a seer, he is never identified as a prophet, even though the narrative in the book of Numbers associates him with the prophetic characteristics of receiving messages from the LORD, delivering messages or oracles under the influence of the LORD, and seeing visions and having knowledge of God Most High.

**Meditation/Journal:** Do you think Balaam is a true prophet or a false prophet? What evidence can you present to defend your position?

**Psalm Response**: "God, mark us with grace / and blessing! Smile! / The whole country will see how you work, / all the godless nations see how you save. / God! Let people thank and enjoy you. / Let all people thank and enjoy you. / You mark us with blessing, O God, our God. / You mark us with blessing, O God." (Ps 67:1–3, 7, TM)

## Barnabas

**Scripture**: ". . . [I]n the church at Antioch there were prophets and teachers: Barnabas . . . and Saul. While they were worshiping the Lord and fasting, the Holy Spirit said, 'Set apart for me Barnabas and Saul for the work to which I have called them.' Then after fasting and praying they laid their hands on them and sent them off." (Acts 13:1–3, NRSVue)

**Reflection**: The author of the CB (NT) Acts of the Apostles introduces Barnabas "(which means 'son of encouragement')" (Acts 4:36, NRSVue), as one who sold a field and brought the money to the apostles (Act 4:37). When he appears later in the narrative, he is identified as a prophet in Antioch, as noted in the above Scripture passage. He accompanies Saul (Paul) on a missionary journey (Acts 13:4—14:28) and to Jerusalem, where a decision is reached about the circumcision of gentiles (Acts 15:1–35), after which they separate (Acts 15:36–41). However, before that occurred, both Barnabas and Paul are named apostles (Acts 14:4, 6, 14) by the author of the Acts of the Apostles; that title is usually reserved for the twelve. Thus, in Christian tradition, Barnabas is considered both a prophet and an apostle.

**Meditation/Journal**: To what work has God called you? Who has encouraged you in your work? Whom have you encouraged in his or her work?

**Psalm Response**: ". . . [M]e [GOD] caught—reached all the way / from sky to sea; he pulled me out / of . . . the void in which I was drowning. . . . / GOD stuck by me. / He stood me up in a wide-open field; / I stood there saved—surprised to be loved! / GOD made my life complete / when I placed all the pieces before him. / Now I'm alert to GOD's ways; / I don't take God for granted." (Ps 18: 16, 18–21, TM)

## Caiaphas

**Scripture**: ". . . Caiaphas, who was high priest . . . , said to [the Jews]: 'You do not understand that it is better for you to have one man die for the people than to have the whole nation destroyed.' He did not say this on his own, but being high priest . . . he prophesied that Jesus was about to die for the nation, and not for the nation only, but to gather into one the dispersed children of God." (John 11:49–52)

**Reflection**: Unique to John's Gospel in the CB (NT) is the prophet Caiaphas, who was high priest from 18 to 36 CE, was both a political and a religious leader. In the passage above, he predicts Jesus' death for all people. The Johannine narrator interprets Caiaphas' words as applying to all God's dispersed children. Later in the gospel, the narrator again reminds the reader, "Caiaphas was the one who had advised the Jews that it was better to have one person die for the people" (John 18:14). Caiaphas echoes a Johannine-Jesus theme about being the good shepherd, who lays down his life for the sheep, and who has other sheep that do not belong to the fold. The goal is one flock with one shepherd (John 10:14–17). After he is lifted up (on the cross and raised from the dead), the Johannine Jesus states that he will draw all people to himself (John 12:32). And in one of his prayers, the Johannine Jesus asks that all believers will be one, as he and the Father are one (John 17:21–22). Thus, in a very parabolic way, Caiphas and Jesus agree on Jesus' mission in John's Gospel: to die for the people and to gather into one all God's children.

**Meditation/Journal**: In your life, who is like the Johannine Caiaphas? Explain.

**Psalm Response**: "Everyone pokes fun at me [, God,]; / they make faces at me, they shake their heads. / 'Let's see how GOD handles this one; / since God likes him so much, let *him* help him!' / I'm a bucket kicked over and spilled, / every joint in my body has been pulled apart. / My heart is a blob / of melted wax in my gut. / I'm dry as a bone, / my tongue black and swollen. / They have laid me out for burial / in the dirt. / You, GOD—don't put off my rescue! / Hurry and help me! (Ps 22:7–8, 14–15, 19, TM)

## Communicator

**Scripture**: Elihu said to Job: ". . . [T]ruly it is the spirit in a mortal, / the breath of the Almighty that makes for understanding. / . . . I am full of words; / the spirit within me constrains me. / I must speak, so that I may find relief; / I must open my lips and answer." (Job 32:8, 18, 20, NRSVue)

**Reflection**: Prophets were excellent communicators. Their words bubbled and overflowed like a fountain. In the HB (OT) book of Job, Elihu attributes his words to the spirit within him; he states that he is compelled to speak. Prophets were inter-communicators between God and people. God revealed to them in thoughts and dreams what he wanted communicated to his people. In other words, biblical prophets breathed God's spirit; they were inspired to disclose God's fundamental truths, no matter if the message was positive or negative. Once they received the message, they could not rest until they delivered it. In common understanding, people define prophets as future-tellers. However, in most cases they were not seers—seeing into the future—but heralds of divine will. In other words, they were like the conscience of the Israelites and, after the kingdom divided, they became the conscience of the nations of Israel and Judah, especially their kings. True prophets were those who witnessed their words come true; false prophets were those whose words failed. The function of prophet that took shape in the HB (OT) continued into the CB (NT).

**Meditation/Journal**: From your perspective, who is a modern prophet? Explain.

**Psalm Response**: "Hallelujah! / Thank GOD! Pray to him by name! / Tell everyone you meet what he has done! / Sing him songs, belt out hymns, / translate his wonders into music! / Honor his holy name with Hallelujahs, / you who seek GOD. Live a happy life! / Keep your eyes open for GOD, watch for his works; / be alert for signs of his presence. / Remember the world of wonders he has made . . . . / [He told kings] 'Don't you dare lay a hand on my anointed, / don't hurt a hair on the heads of my prophets.'" (Ps 105:1–5a, 15, TM)

## Daniel

**Scripture**: Jesus said to his disciples: ". . . [W]hen you see the desolating sacrilege, spoken of by the prophet Daniel, standing in the holy place (let the reader understand), then those in Judea must flee to the mountains; the one on the housetop must not go down to take things from the house; the one in the field must not turn back to get a coat." (Matt 24:15–18, NRSVue)

**Reflection**: The author of Matthew's Gospel copies the above words from Mark's Gospel (13:14–16), except for supplying the source of "the desolating sacrilege" as coming from the HB (OT) prophet Daniel. Daniel mentions "a desolating sacrilege" three times (Dan 9:27; 11:31; 12:11). In Daniel, the "desolating sacrilege" refers to the sacrifice of a pig on the Temple's altar by King Antiochus IV Epiphanes in 167 BCE after erecting a statue of Zeus in the Temple (1 Macc 1:47, 54a, 59; 6:7). According to the HB (OT) book of Deuteronomy, the pig was an unclean animal. In the HB (OT) book of the prophet Daniel, Daniel does not refer to himself as a prophet; it is the author of Matthew's Gospel in the CB (NT) who identifies Daniel as a prophet. For the author of Matthew's Gospel, the words of the prophet Daniel provide to those who understand a prediction of the destruction of the Temple in 70 CE by the Romans, which, of course, had already occurred by the time the author was composing his gospel. By portraying his Jesus character as predicting the future, the author gives him credibility and makes him a prophet.

**Meditation/Journal**: In your life, what recent event was reinterpreted by a family member as having been predicted? Explain.

**Psalm Response**: "I bless GOD every chance I get; / my lungs expand with his praise. / I live and breathe GOD; / if things aren't going well, hear this and be happy. / Join me in spreading the news; / together let's get the word out. / Open your mouth and taste, open your eyes and see—how good GOD is. / Blessed are you who run to him." (Ps 34:1–3, 8, TM)

## David

**Scripture**: Peter said: "Fellow Israelites, I may say to you confidently of our ancestor David that he both died and was buried, and his tomb is with us to this day. Since he was a prophet, he knew that God had sworn with an oath to him that he would put one of his descendants on his throne. Foreseeing this, David spoke of the resurrection of the Messiah . . . ." (Acts 2:29–31, NRSVue)

**Reflection**: The clearest statement that the author of the CB (NT) book of the Acts of the Apostles considered David to be a prophet is found in the speech Peter delivers to the Jews after Pentecost. In the above passage, the author compares the death, burial, and tomb of David to the death, burial, and resurrection of the Messiah. He presumes that the psalms of David were prophecy; David was not singing about himself, but spoke as a prophet of another one, who would fulfill David's words. Furthermore, the author of the Acts of the Apostles considers the Holy Spirit through David to have foretold the events concerning Judas Iscariot (Acts 1:15–20). It is not difficult to see how the author reached his conclusion that David was a prophet. The last words of David, recorded in the HB (OT) Second Book of Samuel, state: "The spirit of the LORD speaks through me; / his word is upon my tongue" (2 Sam 23:2). The author of the Second Book of Samuel declares that David's last words are an oracle (2 Sam 23:1) of one whom God exalted and anointed. Thus, the CB (NT) author of the Acts of the Apostles considers David to have been a prophet.

**Meditation/Journal**: In your family, whom do you consider to be a prophet? Explain.

**Psalm Response**: "A long time ago you [, GOD,] spoke in a vision, / you spoke to your faithful beloved: / 'I've crowned a hero, / I chose the best I could find; / I found David, my servant, / poured holy oil on his head, / And I'll keep my hand steadily on him, / yes, I'll stick with him through thick and thin. / I'm with him for good and I'll love him forever; / I've set him on high—he's riding high! / Yes, I'm setting him apart as the First of the royal line, / High King over all of earth's kings. / I'll preserve him eternally in my love, / I'll faithfully do all I so solemnly promised. / I'll guarantee his family tree / and underwrite his rule.'" (Ps 89:19–21, 24, 27–29, TM)

## Deborah

**Scripture**: ". . . Deborah, a prophet . . . was judging Israel. She used to sit under the palm of Deborah . . . in the hill country . . . , and the Israelites came up to her for judgment." (Judg 4:4–5, NRSVue)

**Reflection**: Deborah is more accurately described as a prophetess. According to the narrative found in the HB (OT) book of Judges, when the Israelites were being oppressed by the Canaanites—King Jabin and Army Commander Sisera—they appealed to Deborah, who summoned Barak to command an Israelite army. However, it was Deborah who gave the order for the Israelite army to engage in battle with the Canaanite army. ". . . [T]he LORD threw Sisera and all his chariots and all his army into a panic before Barak; Sisera got down from his chariot and fled away on foot" (Judg 4:15, NRSVue). Sisera fled to the tent of Jael, who hid him under a rug. Then, taking a tent peg, while he slept, she drove it into his temple, and he died.

**Meditation/Journal**: In your family, who was or is a warrior, prophetic woman, like Deborah? Explain.

**Canticle Response**: ". . . [I]n the time of Jael, / Public roads were abandoned, / travelers went by backroads. / Then you, Deborah, rose up; / you got up, a mother in Israel. / God chose new leaders, / who then fought at the gates. / Wake up, wake up Deborah! / Wake up, wake up, sing a song! / On your feet, Barak! / Most blessed of all women is Jael, / . . . most blessed of homemaking women. / She grabbed a tent peg in her left hand, / with her right hand she seized a hammer. / She hammered Sisera, she smashed his head, / she drove a hole through his temple. / He slumped at her feet. He fell. He sprawled. / He slumped at her feet. He fell. / Slumped. Fallen. Dead." (Judg 5:6b–8a, 12, 24, 26–27, TM)

## Eldad

**Scripture**: ". . . Moses . . . gathered seventy of the elders of the people . . . . Then the LORD came down in the cloud and spoke to him and took some of the spirit that was on him and put it on the seventy elders, and when the spirit rested upon them, they prophesied. Two men remained in the camp, one named Eldad . . . , and the spirit rested on [him]; [he was] among those registered, but [he] had not gone out . . . , so [he] prophesied in the camp. And a young man ran and told Moses, 'Eldad [is] prophesying in the camp.' And Joshua son of Nun, the assistant of Moses, one of his chosen men, said, 'My lord Moses, stop them!' But Moses said to him, 'Are you jealous for my sake?

Would that all of the LORD's people were prophets and that the LORD would put his spirit on them!'" (Num 11:24–25a, 26–29)

**Reflection**: The above Scripture text from the HB (OT) book of Numbers is the only biblical account concerning the prophet Eldad. Not only is nothing else known about him, but the words of his prophecy are not recorded. He is one of seventy-two elders, who are chosen to help govern the Israelites. However, he did not go to the shared-spirit event, but he received some of the spirit of Moses, just like the other elders. After a tattle-tale young man informs Moses about the extra-spirit event, Joshua tells Moses to stop Eldad from prophesying. In response, Moses expresses his wish that God would make all his people prophets by putting his spirit on them. This account of Eldad's reception of the spirit is connected to the story following it about the quails. In Hebrew the word for breath, wind, and spirit is *ruah*. Thus, the *ruah* that prompts Eldad to prophesy is the same *ruah* that goes out from the LORD and brings quails to the Israelite camp (Num 11:31). The breath, wind, and spirit of God cannot be controlled by human beings.

**Meditation/Journal**: What has been your most recent experience of being unable to control the breath, wind, or spirit? Explain.

**Psalm Response**: "[GOD,] Is there anyplace I can go to avoid your Spirit? / to be out of your sight? / If I climb to the sky, you're there! / If I go underground, you're there! / If I flew on morning's wings, / to the far western horizon, / You'd find me in a minute— / you're already there waiting! / Then I said to myself, 'Oh, he even sees me in the dark! / At night I'm immersed in the light!' / It's a fact: darkness isn't dark to you; / night and day, darkness and light, they're all the same to you." (Ps 139:7–12, TM)

## Eliezer

**Scripture**: ". . . King Jehoshaphat of Judah joined with King Ahaziah of Israel, who did wickedly. He joined him in building ships to go to Tarshish . . . . Then Eliezer . . . prophesied against Jehoshaphat, saying, 'Because you have joined with Ahaziah, the LORD will destroy what you have made.' And the ships were wrecked and were not able to go to Tarshish." (2 Chr 20:35–37, NRSVue)

**Reflection**: While there are eleven men named Eliezer in biblical literature, there is only one of them identified as a prophet, as noted in the passage above from the Second Book of Chronicles in the HB (OT). The prophet Eliezer rebukes King Jehoshaphat of Judah (870–848 BCE) for his alliance with King Ahaziah of Israel (853–852 BCE) in an effort to resume commercial fleet operations. In other words, Jehoshaphat in the poorness of the south desired to get in on the flourishing economy of the north. According to Eliezer, God did not approve of the alliance because of the north's idolatry. Jehoshaphat's punishment was the destruction of the means of the alliance: the ships, which had been prepared for the economic venture. Because his prophecy came true, Eliezer is considered a true prophet.

**Meditation/Journal**: Who has prophesied negatively about one of your projects? Explain.

**Psalm Response**: "Some of you set sail in big ships; / you put to sea to do business in faraway ports. / Out at sea you saw GOD in action, / saw his breathtaking ways with the ocean: / With a word he called up the wind— / an ocean storm, towering waves! / You shot high in the sky, then the bottom dropped out; / your hearts were stuck in your throats. / You were spun like a top, you reeled like a drunk, / you didn't know which end was up. / Then you called out to GOD in your desperate condition; / he got you out in the nick of time. / He quieted the wind down to a whisper, / put a muzzle on all the big waves. / And you were so glad when the storm died down, / and he led you safely back to harbor. / So thank GOD for his marvelous love, / for his miracle mercy to the children he loves." (Ps 107:23–31, TM)

## Elihu

**Scripture**: ". . . Elihu had waited to speak to Job because [Job's three friends—Eliphaz, Bildad, and Zophar—] were older than he. . . . Elihu saw that there was no answer in the mouths of these three men . . . . Elihu [said]: '. . . [T]ruly it is the spirit in a mortal, / the breath of the Almighty that makes for understanding. It is not the old who are wise / nor the aged who understand what is right. . . . I am full of words; / the spirit within me constrains me. The spirit of God has made me, / and the breath of the Almighty gives me life.'" (Job 32:4–5, 8–9, 18; 33:4, NRSVue)

**Reflection**: Elihu, the fourth man to address Job in the HB (OT) book of Job, is considered a prophet, because he gives four speeches about God after an introduction (Job 32:1—37:24). Elihu dispels the biblical presupposition that wisdom comes with age. He states that it is the breath (spirit) of God that enables understanding. He, a younger man than Job's three friends, experiences himself being full of inspired words, as any prophet does. The God who made him breathed life into him, even though, like Job and his friends, Elihu has been created from clay (Job 33:6). Elihu states that God speaks in dreams and in visions (Job 33:14–15). He urges Job to listen to him so he can teach

Job wisdom (Job 33:31–33). Because God speaks to his prophet through spirit, Elihu understands that should the divine "take back his spirit to himself / and gather to himself his breath, / all flesh would perish together, / and all mortals return to dust" (Job 34:14–15). While people cannot find God (Job 37:23), they can stop and consider the wondrous works he does (Job 37:14).

**Meditation/Journal**: In your life, what works has God done? How do those works lead you closer to God?

**Psalm Response**: "O God! Your way is holy! / No god is great like God! / You're the God who makes things happen; / you showed everyone what you can do— / Ocean saw you in action, God, / saw you and trembled with fear; / Deep Ocean was scared to death. / Clouds belched buckets of rain, / Sky exploded with thunder, / your arrows flashing this way and that. / From Whirlwind came your thundering voice, / Lightning exposed the world, / Earth reeled and rocked. / You strode right through Ocean, / walked straight through roaring Ocean, / but nobody saw you come or go." (Ps 77:13–14, 16–19, TM)

## Elijah

**Scripture**: "At the time of the offering of the oblation the prophet Elijah came near [to the wood, pieces of bull, stone, and water] and said, 'O LORD, God of Abraham, Isaac, and Israel, let it be known this day that you are God in Israel, that I am your servant, and that I have done all these things at your bidding. Answer me, O LORD, answer me, so that this people may know that you, O LORD, are God and that you have turned their hearts back.' Then the fire of the LORD fell and consumed the burnt offering, the wood, the stones, and the dust and even licked up the water than was in the trench. When all the people saw it, they fell on their faces and said, 'The LORD indeed is God; the LORD indeed is God.'" (1 Kgs 18:36–39, NRSVue)

**Reflection**: The prophet Elijah has no book named after him; his story is narrated in the HB (OT) First Book of Kings (17:1—2 Kgs 2:15). There is a drought in the Northern Kingdom of Israel, announced by Elijah to King Ahab (874–853 BCE); in other words, the drought is affecting the growing economy of Israel. The above passage concludes a dueling-prophets story which determines who the real fertility god is: Baal or the LORD. The 450 prophets of Baal and the single prophet of the LORD—Elijah—meet on Mount Carmel; the astute Bible reader must realize that the LORD lives on mountain tops. Thus, the winner of the duel is already determined! Baal's prophets prepare the sacrificial bull on wood, but their prayer for fire goes unheard. As noted in the passage above, Elijah's prayer is heard. Once the prophets of Baal are killed

(1 Kgs 18:40), the drought ends, further indicating that the LORD is the real fertility God. The acclamation of the people attending the dueling-prophets spectacle makes it clear that the LORD is God.

**Meditation/Journal**: In your life, when have you experienced an event, a discussion, etc. that enabled you to state either to others and/or to yourself that the LORD is God? Explain.

**Canticle Response**: ". . . [T[here arose like a flame a prophet whose word burned like a torch. With the Lord's advice and consent, her turned the rain off and the fire on—blitzing the earth three times. He was, of course, Elijah, and his ability to do miraculous things increased exponentially. Elijah was caught up by a whirlwind, horses of fire pulling his chariot up and away. Like Elijah, we all have only one life to live; unlike him we all have to die and don't have his reputation to leave behind." (Sir 48:1, 3–4a, 9, 11, TM)

## Elisha

**Scripture**: ". . . [Elijah] set out . . . and found Elisha . . . , who was plowing. There were twelve yoke of oxen ahead of him, and he was with the twelfth. Elijah passed by him and threw his mantle over him. He left the oxen, ran after Elijah, and said, 'Let me kiss my father and my mother, and then I will follow you.' He returned from following him, took the yoke of oxen, and slaughtered them; using the equipment from the oxen, he boiled their flesh and gave it to the people; and they ate. Then he set out and followed Elijah and became his servant." (1 Kgs 19:19–20a, 21, NRSVue)

**Reflection**: After killing the prophets of Baal, Elijah travels to Mount Horeb (Sinai), where God speaks to him, telling him to find Elisha and to anoint him as prophet to succeed him (1 Kgs 19:16). As narrated above, Elijah finds Elisha plowing a field with twelve yoke of oxen; the number twelve indicates that he will be the prophet for all the twelve tribes. Taking his mantle, a sign of prophetic office, he wraps Elisha in it; Elisha is now Elijah's replacement prophet. After Elijah is picked up by a chariot of fire pulled by horses of fire and ascends to heaven in a whirlwind (2 Kgs 2:11), Elisha retrieves Elijah's mantle that had fallen from him (2 Kgs 2:13) to indicate not only that he succeeds Elijah, but that he receives the power that Elijah had. Power is demonstrated immediately; Elisha wields Elijah's mantle and strikes the water of the Jordan River, which parts so Elisha can cross on dry land (2 Kgs 2:13–14).

**Meditation/Journal**: In your life and/or work, whom have you succeeded? What power was given to you? Explain.

**Canticle Response**: "Elijah . . . left behind his spirit in Elisha. No one was more powerful than he; no one bested him when faced with word-to-word combat. Alive he did wonders; dead, wonders continued to be attributed to him." (Sir 48:12, 14, TM)

## Elymas (Bar-Jesus)

**Scripture**: "When [Barnabas and Saul (Paul)] had gone through the whole island [of Cyprus] . . . , they met a certain magician, a Jewish false prophet, named Bar-Jesus. But the magician Elymas (for that is the translation of his name) opposed them . . . . But Saul, also known as Paul, filled with the Holy Spirit, looked intently at him and said, '. . . [T]he hand of the Lord is against you, and you will be blind for a while, unable to see the sun.' Immediately mist and darkness came over him, and he fumbled about for someone to lead him by the hand." (Acts 13:6, 8–9, 11, NRSVue)

**Reflection**: Not only does the above passage from the CB (NT) book of the Acts of the Apostles feature Saul (Paul) having the ability to blind a clearly identified false prophet, it also contains some not obvious similarities. For example, both Saul (Paul) and Elymas (Bar-Jesus) are known by more than one name. Paul engages in spiritual warfare; in other words, there is a case of dueling prophets. Paul represents the preaching of the word of God; Elymas represents the opposition to faith, which results from the proclamation. Before his conversion, Paul was blinded for a while, just like he blinds Elymas for a while. Paul was led by the hand, just like Elymas was led by the hand. And, not to be missed is the description of the weather: mist and darkness. In other words, the weather illustrates Elymas' disposition as one who is trying to steer God's word away.

**Meditation/Journal**: In what recent experience of your life has the weather reflected the event in which you were involved? Explain.

**Psalm Response**: "GOD, investigate my life; / get all the facts firsthand. / I'm an open book to you; / even from a distance, you know what I'm thinking. / You know when I leave and when I get back; / I'm never out of your sight. / . . . I said to myself, 'Oh, he even sees me in the dark! / At night I'm immersed in the light!' / It's a fact: darkness isn't dark to you; / night and day, darkness and light, they're all the same to you." (Ps 139:1–3, 11–12, TM)

## Elizabeth

**Scripture**: "When Elizabeth heard Mary's greeting, the child leaped in her womb. And Elizabeth was filled with the Holy Spirit and exclaimed with a loud cry, 'Blessed are you among women, and blessed is the fruit of your womb. And why has this happened to me, that the mother of my Lord comes to me? For as soon as I heard the sound of your greeting, the child in my womb leaped for joy. And blessed is she who believed that there would be a fulfillment of what was spoken to her by the Lord.'" (Luke 1:41–45, NRSVue)

**Reflection**: Elizabeth, the mother of John the Baptizer, is a prophetess, because the author of Luke's Gospel presents her as filled with the Spirit. And just as John the Baptist heralded the appearance of Jesus, Elizabeth heralds the appearance of Mary, Jesus' mother, identifying her as one who believed what the Lord spoke to her, which has come to pass in her womb. John the Baptist leaps in his mother's womb in anticipation of his role to come, while his prophetess-mother is overcome with Spirit and declares the mother of Jesus to be a blessed woman in her faithfulness and in bearing blessed fruit in her womb.

**Meditation/Journal**: During your life, who has declared you faithful or blessed? Explain.

**Canticle Response**: "Blessed are you, O Lord, God of our ancestors! You alone are praiseworthy and high above us, and your name will be blessed forever! / Blessed are you who take time to observe what is going on her below; you are praiseworthy and high above us forever! / Blessed are you for always seeing the big picture; you are praiseworthy and high above us forever. / . . . [P]rophets, bless the Lord, praise and honor him forever." (Dan 3:52, 55–56, 84 [Sg Three 1:29, 32–33, 62], TM)

## Enoch

**Scripture**: ". . . Enoch, in the seventh generation from Adam, prophesied, saying, 'See, the Lord is coming with ten thousands of his holy ones, to execute judgment on all, and to convict all the ungodly of all the deeds of ungodliness that they have committed in such an ungodly way and of all the harsh things that ungodly sinners have spoken against him.'" (Jude 1:14–15, NRSVue)

**Reflection**: Enoch is the son of Cain and his wife (Gen 4:17). However, the HB (OT) book also states that Jared, a descendant of Seth, is the father of Enoch (Gen 5:18), who "walked with God; then he was no more, because God took him" (Gen 5:24), which suggests that Enoch did not die a normal death and takes his place in Jewish tradition as one who walked with God. The passage about Enoch in the CB (NT) Letter of Jude is another instance of a later biblical author designating someone a prophet much later, after his death, in history, when the person in his own time was not named as such. Not only does the anonymous author of the Letter of Jude declare Enoch to be a prophet, but he also quotes from the First Book of Enoch (1:9), which was never included in any collection (canon) of biblical books. In other words, the author of the CB (NT) Letter of Jude considers 1 Enoch 1:9 to be prophecy, and, thus its author, Enoch, to be a prophet.

**Meditation/Journal**: Whom do you know who has been made bigger than life after death than he or she ever was when alive? Explain.

**Psalm Response**: "What can I give back to GOD / for the blessings he's poured out on me? / I'll complete what I promised GOD I'd do, / and I'll do it together with his people. / When they arrive at the gates of death, / GOD welcomes those who love him. / Oh, GOD, here I am, your servant, / your faithful servant: set me free for your service!" (Ps 116:12, 14–16, TM)

## Ezekiel

**Scripture**: "Like the bow in a cloud on a rainy day, such was the appearance . . . of the likeness of the glory of the LORD. He said to me, 'Mortal, I am sending you to the people of Israel . . . and you shall say to them, "Thus says the Lord GOD." Whether they hear or refuse to hear . . . , they shall know that there has been a prophet among them. You shall speak my words to them . . . .' I looked, and a hand was stretched out to me, and a written scroll was in it. He said to me, 'O mortal, eat what is offered to you; eat this scroll, and go speak to the house of Israel.' Then I ate it, and in my mouth it was as sweet as honey. He said to me, 'Mortal, go to the house of Israel and speak my very words to them.'" (Ezek 1:28; 2:3–5, 7, 9; 3:1, 3b–4, NRSVue)

**Reflection**: Ezekiel was a priest, who was deported to Babylon by King Nebuchadnezzar in 597 BCE. He recorded his experiences and prophecies—many of which are enacted—between 593 and 571 BCE. His vision of the LORD—wind, cloud, fire, thunder, light, etc.—contains the typical biblical elements of a theophany, an appearance of God, which Ezekiel compares to a rainbow. God addresses Ezekiel as mortal; older translations stated son of man. He is called by God and sent to the Jewish exiles in Babylon, to where King Nebuchadnezzar had, in his first round of deportations after he captured Jerusalem, taken the boy-king of Judah and his court to Babylon, and established the boy-king's uncle as client king of Jerusalem. According to Ezekiel's prophetic call, it makes no difference whether the Jewish captives listen to him or not; all that matters is that they come to realize that God has not abandoned them, but he has sent his prophet to them. The Lord GOD gives Ezekiel a scroll with writing on both sides; the scroll is the word of God that the LORD wants proclaimed to his people in exile. In order for Ezekiel to get that word inside himself, he must eat the scroll, which was sweet as honey in his mouth. Then, with the word of God inside him, he is able to go to the Jewish exiles and deliver the divine word to them. The prophet lives by the River (Canal) Chebar (Ezek 1:1; 3:15), where the word of God comes to him after seven days: "Mortal, I have made you a sentinel for the house of Israel, whenever you hear a word from my mouth, you shall give them warning from me" (Ezek 3:17, NRSVue).

**Meditation/Journal**: What experience of the LORD have you had? How do you describe it? What word of God has come to you? Explain.

**Psalm Response**: "You're blessed when you stay on course, / walking steadily on the road revealed by GOD. / How can a . . . person live a clean life? / By carefully reading the map of your Word [, GOD]. / I've banked your promises in the vault of my heart . . . / because I trusted your Word. / When they see me waiting, expecting your Word, / those who fear you will take heart and be glad. / Your Word and truth are dependable as ever . . . . / By your words I can see where I'm going; / they throw a beam of light on my dark path." (Ps 119:1, 9, 11a, 42b, 74, 91a, 105, TM)

Biblical Prophets

# F to I

3

# F–I

## FROM FALSE PROPHET TO ISAIAH'S WIFE

### False Prophet

**Scripture**: "The sixth angel poured his bowl on the great River Euphrates, and its water was dried up in order to prepare the way for the kings from the east. And I saw three foul spirits like frogs coming from the mouth of the dragon, from the mouth of the beast, and from the mouth of the false prophet. These are demonic spirits, performing signs, who go abroad to the kings of the whole world, to assemble them for battle on the great day of God the Almighty." (Rev 16:12–14, NRSVue)

**Reflection**: The CB (NT) book of Revelation is built on the number seven, because the number three represents the divine and the number four represents the earth; the sum of three and four is seven, indicating completeness. The sixth of seven angels—all of whom carry bowls of God's wrath—dries the River Euphrates—in order to make a road for the Parthians, successors to the Persians. Next, in his vision the author sees three foul spirits, who are like frogs, which are unclean animals. The three beasts featured in the above passage appeared in chapter 13. The dragon is Satan, the beast from the sea is the emperor, and the beast from the land is the Roman imperial cult enforcer with false prophecy. Later in the narrative, the beast and the false prophet are captured and thrown alive into the lake of fire (Rev 19:20) and the devil (Satan) joins them there shortly thereafter (Rev 20:10). The unclean frogs hearken to the second plague in the HB (OT) book of Exodus (8:1–7). Thus, the author of Revelation likens the enforcers of the Roman imperial cult, along with Satan and the emperor—a trinity of evil—to the unclean frogs of the Exodus! They are presented with the mission of deceiving the kings of the earth. This genre of writing, known as apocalyptic (meaning *revelation*), was designed to offer hope and comfort to those who remained faithful to Jesus Anointed by offering an alternative vision to the one of persecution they were experiencing. In other words, on the great day of God Almighty, the trinity of evil is defeated.

**Meditation/Journal**: In your life, what recent event gave you hope? Explain.

**Canticle Response**: "Mighty your acts and marvelous, / O God, the Sovereign-Strong! / Righteous your ways and true, / King of the nations! / Who can fail to fear you, God, / give glory to your Name? / Because you and you only are holy, / all nations will come and worship you, / because they see your judgments are right. / Righteous you are, and your judgments are righteous, / THE IS, THE WAS, THE HOLY. / Yes, O God, the Sovereign-Strong! / Your judgments are true and just!" (Rev 15:3–4; 16:5, 7, TM)

## Four Daughters

**Scripture**: ". . . [W]e . . . came to Caesarea, and we went into the house of Philip the evangelist, one of the seven, and stayed with him. He had four unmarried daughters who had the gift of prophecy." (Acts 21:8–9, NRSVue)

**Reflection**: The above Scripture passage is part of what biblical scholars refer to as the "we-section" of the CB (NT) Acts of the Apostles. Instead of third-person narrative, the author of the book suddenly begins to use the first-person plural pronoun. While at one time biblical scholars considered that the author was present at the times when he used *we*, today most scholars think that the author had a travel journal that he used as a source for his book from Acts 16:10 to 28:16. From the text it is impossible to determine who the *we* are, since the only antecedent noun is Paul. In Caesarea, they enter the home of Philip, who was one of the seven chosen to serve widows (Acts 6:5), identified in the above biblical passage as an evangelist—based on his activity (Acts 8:4, 40)—with four unmarried daughters possessing the gift of prophecy. It is important to note here that for the author of Luke-Acts, prophetesses are celibate. Also important is the fact that the four prophetesses do not prophecy. Immediately, in the next verse, a male prophet appears. In other words, as early as the end of the first century, there is opposition to prophetesses, even though these four daughters of Philip probably were well known in some communities of believers.

**Meditation/Journal**: What do you think about female prophets (prophetesses)?

**Psalm Response**: "I wonder why you care, GOD— / why do you bother with us at all? / All we are is a puff of air; / we're like shadows in a campfire. / Make our sons in their prime / like sturdy oak trees, / Our daughters as shapely and bright / as fields of wildflowers. / Fill our barns with great harvest, / fill our fields with huge flocks . . . ." (Ps 144:3–4, 12–13, TM)

## Gad

**Scripture**: ". . . [T]he prophet Gad said to David, 'Do not remain in the stronghold [of Mizpeh of Moab]; leave and go into the land of Judah.' So David left and went into the forest . . . ." (1 Sam 22:5, NRSVue)

**Reflection**: The prophet Gad serves David while Saul is king and after David becomes king. As noted in the above Scripture text, he sends David, with whom he shares outlaw status, from Moab back to Judah. In the Second Book of Samuel, after David is king and conducts a census, he delivers God's displeasure with the census to David: "Thus says the LORD: Three things I offer you; choose one of them, and I will do it to you." Gad went to David and asked: "Shall seven years of famine come to you on your land? Or will you flee three months before your foes while they pursue you? Or shall there be three days' pestilence in your land?" (2 Sam 24:13, NRSVue). David advises Gad to seek God's mercy (2 Sam 24:14). Thus, the LORD sends a pestilence on the land for three days (2 Sam 24:15). The chronicler includes the records (writings) of Gad in his list of sources about King David's reign (2 Chr 29:29). While Gad is referred to as a prophet, he is better classified as King David's seer (2 Sam 24:11). As a seer, Gad had the ability to receive visions and guidance from God. In other words, he was a spiritual advisor to the king. After receiving divine revelations, he delivered God's messages to the king, often, as in the case of David, speaking truth to power.

**Meditation/Journal**: In your life, who has served you as a seer, a spiritual advisor? Explain.

**Psalm Response**: "Good people, cheer GOD! / Right-living people sound best when praising. / For GOD's Word is solid to the core; / everything he makes is sound inside and out. / Earth is drenched / in GOD's affectionate satisfaction. / From high in the skies GOD looks around, / he sees all Adam's brood. / From where he sits / he overlooks all us earth-dwellers. / He has shaped each person in turn; / now he watches everything we do." (Ps 33:1. 4–5, 13–15, TM)

## Habakkuk

**Scripture**: "The oracle that the prophet Habakkuk saw. / O LORD, how long shall I cry for help, and you will not listen? / Or cry to you 'Violence!' / and you will not save? / Why do you make me see wrongdoing / and look at trouble? / Destruction and violence are before me; / strife and contention arise. / So the law becomes slack, / and justice never prevails. / The wicked surround the righteous; / therefore judgment comes forth perverted." (Hab 1:1–4, NRSVue)

**Reflection**: The work of the prophet Habakkuk is one that can be passed over easily in biblical literature; it consists of only three chapters and doesn't even fill three complete pages in most Bibles. The book begins with the prophet's lament about injustices in Judean society between 609 and 598 BCE. For Habakkuk, destruction and violence describe the ruthless accumulation of wealth, while strife and contention describe the breakdown in Judah's legal and judicial systems. In other words, from Habakkuk's perspective, the wicked are greater in power than the righteous, and, thus, judgment is biased toward the wicked. According to Habakkuk, the LORD tells him that he is rousing the Chaldeans (Babylonians) to punish the Judeans (Hab 1:5–11). Indeed, the Babylonians came to world power from 605 to 562 BCE under the reign of King Nebuchadnezzar II.

**Meditation/Journal**: In your life, what do you consider to be one experience of wickedness triumphing righteousness? How was the LORD involved?

**Prayer Response**: "GOD, I've heard what our ancestors say about you, / and I'm stopped in my tracks, down on my knees. / Do among us what you did among them. / Work among us as you worked among them. / And as you bring judgment, as you surely must, / remember mercy. / GOD's on his way again, / retracing the old salvation route . . . ." (Hab 3:2–3a, TM)

## Haggai

**Scripture**: ". . . [T]he word of the LORD came by the prophet Haggai . . . : 'Thus says the LORD of hosts: These people say the time has not yet come to rebuild the LORD's house.' Then the word of the LORD came by the prophet

Haggai, saying, 'Is it time for you yourselves to live in your paneled houses, while this house lies in ruins?' Now therefore thus says the LORD of hosts: . . . 'Go up to the hills and bring wood and build the house, so that I may take pleasure in it and be honored, says the LORD.'" (Hag 1:1–5a, 7b–8, NRSVue)

**Reflection**: Like Habakkuk above, the prophet Haggai is a very short prophetic book consisting of only two chapters and printed on a page and a half in most Bible. Haggai's main concern in his short work is the reconstruction of the Jerusalem Temple, which was reduced to ruins by King Nebuchadnezzar of Babylon in 586/587 BCE. Haggai writes in 520 BCE, after the exile (587–538 BCE) ended, and Jews began to return to Jerusalem. They are under the reign of the third Persian King Darius; thus, after twenty years, the Jews in Jerusalem had not yet begun the rebuilding of the Temple. After Haggai's preaching, work began and was completed five years later in 515 BCE. It is Haggai's contention that the poor harvests and depressed economy are the result of the Jews' disregard for their religious life, at which center was the Temple. Haggai records the LORD telling him to tell the people, "Because my house lies in ruins, while all of you hurry off to your own houses. Therefore the heavens above you have withheld the dew, and the earth has withheld its produce" (Hag 1:9c–10, NRSVue). After presenting God's displeasure, ". . . Haggai, the messenger of the LORD, spoke to the people with the LORD's message, saying, 'I am with you, says the LORD'" (Hag 1:13, NRSVue)

**Meditation/Journal**: If you were one of the Jews returned from exile and living in Jerusalem, what would be your response to the prophet Haggai's words?

**Psalm Response**: "I'm asking GOD for one thing; / only one thing: / To live with him in his house / my whole life long. / I'll contemplate his beauty; / I'll study at his feet. / That's the only quiet, secure place / in a noisy world, / The perfect getaway, / far from the buzz of traffic. / I'm headed for his place to offer anthems / that will raise the roof! / Already I'm singing God-songs; / I'm making music to GOD." (Ps 27:4–5, 6bc)

## Hanani

**Scripture**: ". . . [T]he seer Hanani came to King Asa of Judah and said to him, 'Because you relied on the king of Aram and did not rely on the LORD your God, the army of the king of Aram has escaped you. For the eyes of the LORD range throughout the entire earth to strengthen those whose heart is true to him. You have done foolishly in this, for from now on you will have wars.'" (2 Chr 16:7, 9, NRSVue)

**Reflection**: The prophet Hanani makes only one appearance in biblical literature. In the passage above from the Second Book of Chronicles, he is identified as a seer, a prophet serving as spiritual advisor to King Asa of Judah (911–870 BCE). Asa's forty-one-year reign was characterized by his removal of idolatry—fertility cults—from Judah. He even removed his mother from her position as queen mother because she was involved in making an image (2 Chr 15:16). According to the chronicler, Asa made a mistake in making an alliance with King Ben-hadad of Aram, after King Baasha of Israel (909–886 BCE) had invaded Judah; instead of relying on the LORD God, he relied on the alliance he had made with Ben-hadad. After delivering the words of God's displeasure with Asa, Asa ordered the prophet Hanani put in stocks and then in prison (2 Chr 16:10). After Asa experienced some kind of feet disease, he again relied on physicians and not on the LORD; then he died (2 Chr 16:11–14). The chronicler concludes that King Asa's fall (death) was due to his reliance upon others instead of total reliance upon God.

**Meditation/Journal**: Do you think that making an alliance with another or relying on physicians is a sign of not trusting (seeking, relying) on God? Explain.

**Prayer Response**: "O GOD, you aren't impressed by numbers or intimidated by a show of force once you decide to help: Help us, O GOD, we have come out to meet this huge army because we trust in you and who you are. Don't let mere mortals stand against you!" (2 Chr 14:11, TM)

## Hananiah

**Scripture**: ". . . [A]t the beginning of the reign of King Zedekiah of Judah, . . . the prophet Hananiah . . . spoke to [Jeremiah] in the house of the LORD . . . , saying, 'Thus says the LORD of hosts, the God of Israel: I have broken the yoke of the king of Babylon. Within two years I will bring back to this place all the vessels of the LORD's house, which King Nebuchadnezzar of Babylon took away from this place and carried to Babylon. I will also bring back to this place King Jeconiah . . . of Judah and all the exiles from Judah who went to Babylon, says the LORD, for I will break the yoke of the king of Babylon.'" (Jer 28:1–4, NRSVue)

**Reflection**: Easily confused with the prophet Hanani is the prophet Hananiah (one of fourteen men bearing that name in biblical literature), who served King Zedekiah (597–586 BCE), whom King Nebuchadnezzar of Babylon had established as a client king once he conquered Jerusalem and took King Jeconiah (Jehoiachin, 597 BCE), who had reigned only three months in Judah, as a captive to Babylon. When Zedekiah began to reign, the prophet Jeremiah had been instructed by God to make and wear a yoke of wood to signify that Judah was under the yoke of Babylon (Jer 27:1–22). The prophet Hananiah disagreed with Jeremiah; he prophesized that within two years the LORD would break the yoke of Babylon and the people of Judah would return with their rightful king and the Temple vessels taken by Nebuchadnezzar. After listening to Hananiah, Jeremiah expressed hope that the LORD would do what Hananiah had said (Jer 28:6). Then, Hananiah smashed the yoke of wood that was around Jeremiah's neck to indicate that the Babylonian yoke had been broken by the LORD (Jer 28:10). Later, the word of the LORD came to Jeremiah: "Go, tell Hananiah, Thus says the LORD: You have broken wooden bars only to forge iron bars in place of them! For thus says the LORD of hosts, the God of Israel: I have put an iron yoke on the neck of all these nations so that they may serve King Nebuchadnezzar of Babylon, and they shall indeed serve him" (Jer 28:13–14, NRSVue). Within a year the prophet Hananiah was dead and declared to be a false prophet, because his words did not come true (Jer 28:9).

**Meditation/Journal**: In your life, whom would you consider to be a false prophet, like Hananiah, whose words spoken to you did not come true? Explain.

**Prayer Response**: "This is a Message from GOD-of-the-Angel-Armies, the God of Israel . . . : 'I'm the one who made the earth, man and woman, and all the animals in the world. I did it on my own without asking anyone's help and I hand it out to whomever I will. Here and now I give all these lands over to my servant Nebuchadnezzar king of Babylon. I have made even the wild animals subject to him. All nations will be under him, then his son, and then his grandson. Then his country's time will be up and the tables will be turned: *Babylon* will be the underdog servant. So don't for a minute listen to all your prophets and spiritualists and fortunetellers, who claim to know the future and who tell you not to give in to the king of Babylon. They're handing you a line of lies, barefaced lies, that will end up putting you in exile far from home.'" (Jer 27:4–7, 9–10a)

## Hosea

**Scripture**: "When the LORD first spoke through Hosea, the LORD said to Hosea, 'Go, take for yourself a wife of prostitution and have children of prostitution, for the land commits great prostitution by forsaking the LORD.' So he went and took Gomer . . . , and she conceived and bore him a son." (Hos 1:2–3, NRSVue)

**Reflection**: Hosea, who has a book named after him in the HB (OT), is a prophet in the Kingdom of Israel during the reign of Jeroboam II (782–753 BCE). His primary image for Israel's disloyalty to God is prostitution. His audience, primarily men, were shamed if their wives were discovered to be prostitutes. Thus, Hosea shocks them into seeing the seriousness of their idolatry by comparing the men to prostitutes! God is depicted as the husband of Israel, his faithless and promiscuous wife. Hosea enacts the message he wishes to deliver to Israel: Just as the wife he marries has been promiscuous, seeking out other lovers, so Israel has been unfaithful to its LORD, seeking other gods to worship. The prophet makes the people aware of their idolatry (prostitution), predicts God's punishment, and expresses hope for renewal. In the Scripture passage above, that hope for renewal is incarnated in Hosea's life through God's directive that he take a wife, who has served as a prostitute; thus, he demonstrates that the land of Israel has been prostituting itself in idolatry before Baal, but he also becomes a sign of God's forgiveness, for his wife, Gomer, conceives and bears him a son; there is hope, if Israel repents. At the time Hosea is composing his book, Israel is under threat of Assyrian expansion, and the prophet sees this as God's way of punishing the Israelites for their infidelity. Israel fell to the Assyrians in 721 BCE. Modern readers must be careful with Hosea's imagery, as it can lead to the condemnation of women and mistreatment of them.

**Meditation/Journal**: What do you consider the positive and the negative consequences of Hosea's imagery? Explain.

**Psalm Response**: "Our God is in heaven / doing whatever he wants to do. / [The nations'] gods are metal and wood, / handmade in a basement shop: / Carved mouths that can't talk, / painted eyes that can't see, / Tin ears that can't hear, / molded noses that can't smell, / Hands that can't grasp, feet that can't walk or run, / throats that never utter a sound. / Those who make them have become just like them, / have become just like the gods they trust." (Ps 115:3–8, TM)

## Hulda

**Scripture**: "When . . . [King Josiah] heard the words of the book of the law, [he said,] 'Go, inquire of the LORD for me, for the people, and for all Judah, concerning the words of this book that has been found . . . .' [They] went to the prophet Hulda . . . . She declared to them, 'Thus says the LORD, the God of Israel: . . . I will indeed bring disaster on this place and on its inhabitants—all the words of the book that the king of Judah has read.'" (2 Kgs 22:11, 13, 14a, 15–16)

**Reflection**: Josiah, King of Judah (640–608 BCE), is declared by the author of the Second Book of Kings to have done what was right in the sight of the LORD (2 Kgs 22:2). During the eighteenth year of his reign, the book of the law of the LORD—most likely the HB (OT) book of Deuteronomy—was found in the Temple. After King Josiah was informed of its contents, he concluded that the people had not been keeping it, and the lack of obedience would trigger God's punishment. Those who had found it went to the prophetess Hulda, who confirmed that disaster was imminent for Jerusalem and Judah. According to her words, the people had fallen into idolatry; they were making offerings to other gods (2 Kgs 22:17). Hulda, one of the few biblical prophetesses, anticipates the destruction of Jerusalem and the Babylonian exile; that was easy for the character of Hulda to do if this part of Second Kings was written after the exile! Hulda also delivers a message for King Josiah (2 Kgs 22:18–20).

**Meditation/Journal**: Whom do you consider to be a prophetess today? What message has she delivered that has affected you?

**Psalm Response**: "Open my eyes [, O LORD,] that I may behold / wondrous things out of your law. / The law of your mouth is better to me / than thousands of gold and silver pieces. / Let your mercy come to me, that I may live, / for your law is my delight. / Oh, how I love your law! / It is my meditation all day long. / Great peace have those who love your law; / nothing can make them stumble." (Ps 119:18, 72, 77, 97, 165, NRSVue)

## Iddo

**Scripture**: "The rest of the acts of [King] Abijah, his behavior and his deeds, are written in the story of the prophet Iddo." (2 Chr 13:22, NRSVue)

**Reflection**: The prophet Iddo is cited by the author of the Second Book of Chronicles as a source, but none of Iddo's words are recorded except in the named sources, which no longer exist! The first mention by the chronicler of Iddo is like the last found in the Scripture verse above. "Now the rest of the acts of Solomon, from first to last," states the chronicler, "are they not written in . . . the visions of the seer Iddo concerning Jeroboam . . . ?" (2 Chr 9:29, NRSVue) Solomon reigned from 970 to 930 BCE. Jeroboam succeeded him as King of Israel from 931 to 910 BCE. In Judah, Rehoboam succeeded Solomon from 931 to 913 BCE. The chronicler's second mention of Iddo asks, "Now the acts of Rehoboam, from first to last, are they not written in the records of . . . the seer Iddo, recorded by genealogy?" (2 Chr 12:15, NRSVue) In the earlier references to Iddo, he is identified as a seer, one gifted with the ability to receive divine visions and give guidance to the king, but in the last reference, Iddo is identified as a prophet. Since all biblical literature discloses about Iddo is found above, he seems to be a prophet, who receives divine revelation that he records concerning kings. However, none of his records remain.

**Meditation/Journal**: In your life, who has been like Iddo, mentioned by others but never really known by you?

**Psalm Response**: "God is magnificent; he can never be praised enough. / There are no boundaries to his greatness. / Generation after generation stands in awe of your work; / each one tells stories of your mighty acts. / Your marvelous doings are headline news; / I could write a book full of the details of your greatness. / GOD is good to one and all; / everything he does is suffused with grace. / My mouth is filled with GOD's praise. / Let everything living bless him, / bless his holy name from now to eternity!" (Ps 145:3–4, 6, 21, TM)

## Isaac

**Scripture**: "The LORD appeared to Isaac and said, 'Do not go down to Egypt . . . . Reside in this land as an alien, and I will be with you and will bless you, for to you and to your descendants I will give all these lands, and I will fulfill the oath that I swore to your father Abraham.'" (Gen 26:2–3, NRSVue)

**Reflection**: Isaac, whose name means *laughter*, is counted among the prophets because, according to the HB (OT) book of Genesis, the LORD appeared to him. Most of the biblical stories with Isaac, son of Abraham and Sarah, in them are, really, either about his father or his sons, Esau and Jacob. Furthermore, the stories in Genesis 26, from where the above Scripture passage is taken, are imitations of stories about Abraham. This makes Isaac a shadowy figure; this means that little is known about him. His name, when mentioned, is often found between Abraham and Jacob: Abraham, Isaac, and Jacob. The covenant God made with Abraham and his descendants is inherited by Isaac and passed on to Jacob. Isaac enacted the words spoken to him by the LORD staying where he was and about receiving blessings from him. The author of Genesis writes: "Isaac sowed seed in that land and in the same year reaped a hundredfold. The LORD blessed him, and the man became rich; he prospered more and more until he became very wealthy" (Gen 26:12–13, NRSVue).

**Meditation/Journal**: What words have you heard from God and enacted? Explain.

**Psalm Response**: "Blessed are you who enter in GOD's name— / from GOD's house we bless you! / GOD is God, / he has bathed us in light. / Festoon the shrine with garlands, / hang colored banners above the altar! / You're my God, and I thank you. / O my God, I lift high your praise. / Thank GOD—he's so good. / His love never quits! (Ps118:26–29, TM)

## Isaiah 1

**Scripture**: "When the servants of King Hezekiah came to [the prophet] Isaiah, Isaiah said to them, 'Say to your master: Thus says the LORD: Do not be afraid because of the words that you have heard, with which the servants of the king of Assyria have reviled me. I myself will put a spirit in him so that he shall hear a rumor and return to his own land; I will cause him to fall by the sword in his own land.'" (2 Kgs 19:5–7, NRSVue)

**Reflection**: The Isaiah mentioned above is found in the HB (OT) Second Book of Kings. King Sennacherib of Assyria entered Judah in 701 BCE during the reign of King Hezekiah (716–687 BCE). Sennacherib demanded tribute of a large amount of silver and gold from Hezekiah, which he paid. But Sennacherib of Assyria was not satisfied; he wanted Hezekiah to surrender Jerusalem and become his client king. Sennacherib's representative advised Hezekiah that his reliance on the LORD God to deliver him would not happen (2 Kgs 18:22, 33). Hezekiah's representatives went to the prophet (2 Kgs 19:2) Isaiah, who told them that the LORD would remain faithful to Hezekiah and Jerusalem (above Scripture passage). Later, Isaiah tells Hezekiah: ". . . [T]hus says the LORD concerning the king of Assyria: He shall not come into this city . . . . For I will defend this city to save it, for my own sake and for the sake of my servant David" (2 Kgs 19:32, 34, NRSVue). Then, the narrator states: "That very night the angel of the LORD set out and stuck down one hundred eighty-five thousand in the camp of the Assyrians; when morning dawned, they were all dead bodies. Then King Sennacherib of Assyria left [and] went home . . ." (2 Kgs 19:35–36). While living in Nineveh, he was killed with a sword in 681 BCE (2 Kgs 19:37). In other words, Isaiah's prophecy came true.

**Meditation/Journal**: From what has God saved you? Who was prophet to you?

**Prayer Response**: "GOD, God of Israel, seated / in majesty on the cherubim-throne, / You are the one and only God, / sovereign over all kingdoms of earth, / Maker of heaven, / maker of earth. / Open your ears, GOD, and listen, / open your eyes and look. / . . . [N]ow O GOD, *our* God, / save us . . . ; / Make all the kingdoms on earth know / that you are GOD, the one and only God." (2 Kgs 19:15–16, 19, TM)

## Isaiah 2 (of Jerusalem)

**Scripture**: "In the year that King Uzziah died, I [, Isaiah,] saw the Lord sitting on a throne, high and lofty, and the hem of his robe filled the temple. Seraphs were in attendance above him; each had six wings: with two they covered their faces, and with two they covered their feet, and with two they flew. And one called to another and said, 'Holy, holy, holy is the LORD of hosts; / the whole earth is full of his glory.'" (Isa 6:1–3, NRSVue)

**Reflection**: Biblical scholars divide the HB (OT) book of the prophet Isaiah into three distinct authors. The first part, Isaiah 1–39, is attributed to Isaiah of Jerusalem, who was active during the reign of King Uzziah (Azariah) (767–740 BCE). Some Bibles further divide Isaiah 1–39 into sections presenting a general introduction (1–4), warnings to Jerusalem and its royal house (5–12), addresses to foreign nations (13–27), and threats to Jerusalem (28–39); these subdivisions are usually based on topics grouped together and presented in the book. The theophany described in Isaiah 6:1–8 also contains the prophet's call and commission. Commonly referred to as a call narrative, it consists of four parts: (1) the appearance of a divine being; Isaiah sees the Lord seated on a throne with the hem of his robe filling the temple with the presence of singing, six-winged seraphs (Isa 6:1–3); (2) an excuse is made; Isaiah states that he is a man of unclean lips (Isa 6:5); (3) an event puts aside the excuse; a seraph removes a live coal from the altar and touches Isaiah lips with it to blot out his uncleanness (Isa 6:6–7); and (4) a charge for mission is given; upon hearing the Lord ask, "Whom shall I send, and who will go for us?" Isaiah raises his hand and says, "Here am I; send me!" (Isa 6:8). Then the Lord tells Isaiah what he wants him to say. Other elements of a biblical theophany are the shaking of the pivots of the temple's threshold (earthquake) and the filling of the temple with smoke (fire) (Isa 6:4; Exod 19:16–25). Taken together the elements of Isaiah's vision present a manifestation of the LORD.

**Meditation/Journal**: Identify a theophany that you experienced (such as a sunrise, the ocean, mountains, the birth of a child, etc.). What elements of the theophany made you aware that it was an appearance of God?

**Psalm Response**: "GOD rules. On your toes, everybody! / He rules from his angel throne—take notice! / GOD looms majestic . . . , / He towers in splendor over all the big names. / Great and terrible your beauty; let everyone praise you! / Holy. Yes, holy. / Lift high GOD, our God; worship at his holy mountain. / Holy. Yes, holy is GOD our God." (Ps 99:1–3, 9, TM)

## Isaiah 3 (Second Isaiah)

**Scripture**: "Thus says the LORD to his anointed, to Cyrus, / whose right hand I have grasped / to subdue nations before him / and to strip kings of their robes, / to open doors before him— / and the gates shall not be closed . . . . I call you by your name; / I give you a title, though you do not know me. / I am the LORD, and there is no other; / besides me there is no god. / I arm you, though you do not know me, / so that they may know, from the rising of the sun / and from the west, that there is no / one beside me; / I am the LORD, and there is no other." (Isa 45: 1, 4b–6, NRSVue)

**Reflection**: Second Isaiah consists of chapters 40 through 55. This prophet Isaiah writes about ten years before the collapse of Babylon before 538 BCE (between 550 and 539 BCE). The prophet is focused on the rise of Cyrus, King of Persia, who conquered Babylon. There is a promise that the Jews exiled in Babylon will return to Judah and Jerusalem. Second Isaiah considers Cyrus to be the LORD's shepherd, who will carry out all God's purpose—to rebuild Jerusalem and the temple (Isa 44:28). In the Scripture passage above, Isaiah refers to Cyrus as the LORD's anointed. Both the title shepherd and the title anointed are used biblically of Israelite kings. Thus, Second Isaiah considers that even a foreign and pagan ruler, who attained world power, did so as the agent of the God of Israel, who directs the course of history to fulfill his promise to set free his people and bring them back to Jerusalem. While Cyrus may not be a worshiper of the LORD, the God of Judah, Second Isaiah records the LORD saying, "I am the LORD, who made all things, / who alone stretched out the heavens, / who by myself spread out the earth" (Isa 44:24b, NRSVue). In other words, according to Second Isaiah, God is in charge. "I have aroused Cyrus in righteousness," states the LORD, "and I will make all his paths straight; / he shall build my city / and set my exiles free, / not for price or reward, / says the LORD of hosts" (Isa 45:13, NRSVue).

**Meditation/Journal**: Identify someone of your people (family, tribe, small group, social group, class, etc.) whom you recognize as one of God's agents. What message did he or she bring to you?

**Psalm Response**: "God is well-known in Judah; / in Israel, he's a household name. / Oh, how bright you shine! / God stands tall and makes things right, / he saves all the wretched on earth. / Instead of smoldering rage—God-praise!

/ All that sputtering rage—now a garland for God! / Do for GOD what you said you'd do— / he is, after all, your God." (Ps 76:1, 4a, 9–11, TM)

## Isaiah 4 (Third Isaiah)

**Scripture**: "Rejoice with Jerusalem, and be glad for her, / all you who love her; / rejoice with her in joy, / all you who mourn over her— / that you may nurse and be satisfied / from her consoling breast, / that you may drink deeply with delight / from her glorious bosom. / For thus says the LORD: / I will extend prosperity to her like a river, / and the wealth of the nations like an overflowing stream, / and you shall nurse and be carried on her arm, / and bounced on her knees. / As a mother comfort her child, / so I will comfort you; / you shall be comforted in Jerusalem." (Isa 66:10–13, NRSVue)

**Reflection**: Biblical scholars detect a third prophet Isaiah in chapters 56 to 66, written sometime after 539 BCE. While these chapters may have individual authors, they presume (an) author(s) resident in Jerusalem or Judah. Even though Jerusalem had been destroyed by the Babylonian King Nebuchadnezzar, God's promise of blessing remained. The message of hope is presented by Third Isaiah using the image of Jerusalem as the mother of the Jews. Even though they are still mourning over her destruction, they are invited, like a baby, to suck with delight at her breasts. Those returning from exile will discover wealth that flows like a river. And, like a child, carried in his or her mother's arms and bounced on his or her mother's knees, the people will be divinely comforted. In other words, there is a glory that is about to descend upon Jerusalem; the first stages of the return and restoration had begun around 520–500 BCE; those who returned first and saw the destruction of Jerusalem and the city's walls were not only overwhelmed by the work needing to be done, but they were struggling to reestablish their identity. Third Isaiah offers them hope of accomplishing those goals; soon the LORD's salvation would come, and his deliverance would be revealed (Isa 56:1).

**Meditation/Journal**: What image do you use to demonstrate the concept of comfort?

**Psalm Response**: "GOD, my shepherd! / I don't need a thing. / You have bedded me down in lush meadows, / you find me quiet pools to drink from. / True to your word, / you let me catch my breath / and send me in the right direction. / Your trusty shepherd's crook / makes me feel secure. / Your beauty and love chase after me / every day of my life. / I'm back home in the house of GOD / for the rest of my life." (Ps 23:1–3, 4c, 6, TM)

## Isaiah's wife

**Scripture**: ". . . [T]he LORD said to me [, Isaiah], 'Take a large tablet and write on it in common characters, "Belonging to Maher-shalal-hash-baz," and have it attested for me by reliable witnesses . . .' And I went to the prophetess, and she conceived and bore a son. Then the LORD said to me, 'Name him Maher-shalal-hash-baz, for before the child knows how to call "My father" or "My mother," . . . the spoil of Samaria will be carried away by the king of Assyria.'" (Isa 8:1–4, NRSVue)

**Reflection**: The prophet Isaiah engages in a double prophetic enactment. He takes a tablet or a large piece of scroll and writes "Hurry-plunder!-Hasten-booty" (the translation of Maher-shalal-hash-baz) on it. The document is then sealed and witnessed. Isaiah is certain that Assyria will be the agent for God's destruction of the Northern Kingdom of Israel, whose capital was Samaria. Then, after taking care of the document, Isaiah has intercourse with his wife, identified as the prophetess; she conceived and bore a son. The LORD instructed Isaiah to name his son "Hurry-plunder!-Hasten-booty." Before the boy was old enough to speak "Daddy" or "Mommy," Israel would be plundered by Assyria, according to the LORD. Because little information is given in the text, the prophetess, Isaiah's wife, may have been an unnamed prophetess in her own right. The boy's name written on the document and given to him is a sign of the Assyrian invasion to come. Both the sealed document and the boy are material representations of Isaiah's prophecy. It is important to note that time—months and years—are ignored or absorbed in the four verses; for example, there is no reference to the time between conception and birth. The Southern Kingdom of Judah had no reason to fear prosperous Israel, because in less than two years (722 BCE), Israel would disappear forever from the face of the earth.

**Meditation/Journal**: What is the meaning of your name? What is the meaning of the names of other people in your family? How does each person's name, yours included, reflect some aspect of the person bearing the name?

**Psalm Response**: "Watch this: God's eye is on those who respect him, / the ones who are looking for his love. / He's ready to come to their rescue in bad times; / in lean times he keeps body and soul together. / We're depending on GOD; / he's everything we need. / What's more, our hearts brim with joy / since we've taken for our own his holy name. / Love us, GOD, with all you've got— / that's what we're depending on." (Ps 33:18–22, TM)

# 4

# J

## FROM JACOB TO JUDAS BARSABBAS

### Jacob

**Scripture**: "Taking one of the stones of the place [to which he had come, Jacob] put it under his head and lay down in that place. And he dreamed that there was a stairway set up on the earth, the top of it reaching to heaven, and the angels of God were ascending and descending on it. And the LORD stood beside him and said, 'I am the LORD, the God of Abraham your [grand]father and the God of Isaac . . . . Know that I am with you and will keep you wherever you go and will bring you back to this land, for I will not leave you until I have done what I have promised you.' Then Jacob woke from his sleep and said, 'Surely the LORD is in this place—and I did not know it. How awesome is this place! This is none other than the house of God, and this is the gate of heaven.'"(Gen 28:11b–13, 15–17, NRSVue)

**Reflection**: The patriarch Jacob, son of Isaac, grandson of Abraham, is considered a prophet because he experienced in a dream a direct revelation of God. The stairway from earth to heaven unites two levels of the three-storied universe; it serves as a physical connection from the earth, where people live, to the heavens, where the LORD and his angelic servants live. In his dream,

Jacob saw the LORD, who had descended the stairway, standing beside him, identifying himself to Jacob, and repeating the promises he made to Abraham and Isaac that are now promises made to Jacob. When they are fulfilled, Jacob will be the living proof that the LORD keeps his word. In the meantime, after awakening Jacob recognizes that a theophany, a manifestation, of God had taken place; that is why the text states that the place where Jacob dreamed was God's house; in other words, it was a place where God lived on the earth; it was a buildingless building! After getting up, Jacob took oil and anointed the stone that was under his head and named the place Bethel, which means *house of God*. The act of anointing the stone with oil identified it as a sacred or holy place on earth. Later in Israelite history, kings of Judah and Israel will be anointed with oil to indicate that they have been called to their office by God. And, in the CB (NT) Jesus will be identified as Messiah (Hebrew for *Anointed*) and Christ (Greek for *Anointed*).

**Meditation/Journal**: Where on the earth do you identify a sacred or holy place? In your life, what occurred there? Explain.

**Psalm Response**: "What a beautiful home, GOD-of-the-Angel-Armies! / I've always longed to live in a place like this, / Always dreamed of a room in your house, / where I could sing for joy to God-alive! / GOD-of-the-Angel-Armies, listen: / O God of Jacob, open your ears—I'm praying! / Look at . . . our faces, shining with your gracious anointing. / One day spent in your house, this beautiful place of worship, / beats thousands spent on Greek island beaches." (Ps 84:1–2, 8–10, TM)

## Jahaziel

**Scripture**: ". . . [T]he spirit of the LORD came upon Jahaziel . . . . He said, 'Listen, all Judah and inhabitants of Jerusalem and King Jehoshaphat: Thus says the LORD to you: Do not fear or be dismayed at this great multitude, for the battle is not yours but God's. This battle is not for you to fight; take your position, stand still, and see the victory of the LORD on your behalf, O Judah and Jerusalem.'" (2 Chr 20:14, 15, 17a, NRSVue)

**Reflection**: Jehoshaphat is king of Judah from 870 to 848 BCE. After hearing that a large army is marching in his direction, he proclaims a fast throughout Judah and prays. The prophet Jahaziel, meaning *God sees*, is overcome with the LORD's spirit; he reminds the king and the people that the imminent battle is not theirs; the battle belongs to the LORD. Jehoshaphat trusts Jahaziel. After preparing for battle, he tells his troops: "Believe in the LORD your God and you will be established; believe his prophets and you will succeed" (2

Chr 20:20b, NRSVue). Instead of fighting, singing occurs, and "the LORD set an ambush against . . . [all] who had come against Judah, so that they were routed" (2 Chr 20:22). In other words, Jahaziel's prophecy came true.

**Meditation/Journal**: When have you predicted something important to happen and watched as it came true? Explain.

**Prayer Response**: "O GOD, God of our ancestors, are you not God in heaven above and ruler of all kingdoms below? You hold all power and might in your fist—no one stands a chance against you! [Your people] have lived here and built a holy house of worship to honor you, saying 'When the worst happens—whether war or flood or disease or famine—and we take our place before this Temple (we know you are personally present in this place!) and pray out our pain and trouble, we know that you will listen and give victory.'" (2 Chr 20:6, 8–9, TM)

## Jehu

**Scripture**: "The word of the LORD came to Jehu . . . against Baasha, saying, 'Since I exalted you out of the dust and made you leader over my people Israel, and you have walked in the way of Jeroboam and have caused my people Israel to sin, provoking me to anger with their sins, therefore I will consume Baasha and his house, and I will make your house like the house of Jeroboam . . . . Moreover, the word of the LORD came by the prophet Jehu . . . against Baasha and his house, . . . because of all the evil that he did in the sight of the LORD . . . . (1 Kgs 16:1–3, 7, NRSVue)

**Reflection**: The prophet Jehu prophesizes in both the Northern Kingdom of Israel and in the Southern Kingdom of Judah. As found in the above Scripture passage, he tells King Baasha, the third king of Israel (909–886 BCE), that the LORD is displeased with him, like the LORD was displeased with the first king of Israel, Jeroboam (931–910 BCE), and intends to wipe out the line of his descendants. Thus, while Elah (886–885 BCE), Baasha's son, inherited the throne from his father, his servant Zimri, commander of half his chariots, conspired against him and killed him and all his brothers (1 Kgs 16:8–9, 11) "according to the word of the LORD, which he had spoken against Baasha by the prophet Jehu" (1 Kgs 16:12, NRSVue). Zimri (885 BCE) places himself on the throne of Israel, but lives for only seven days; Omri, commander of the army, succeeded him (1 Kgs 16:16). In the Southern Kingdom of Judah, "Jehu . . . the seer went out to meet [King Jehoshaphat (870–848 BCE)] and said to King Jehoshaphat, 'Should you help the wicked and love those who hate the LORD? Because of this, wrath has gone out against you from the LORD.

Nevertheless, some good is found in you, for you destroyed the sacred poles out of the land and have set your heart to seek God'"(2 Chr 19:2–3, NRSVue). After listening to Jehu's words, King Jehoshaphat made himself visible to his people and brought many of them back to the LORD (2 Chr 19:4) and initiated many reforms in Jerusalem (2 Chr 19:5–11).

**Meditation/Journal**: During your life, whom have you considered to be a reformer? Explain.

**Psalm Response**: "Listen, Shepherd, Israel's Shepherd— / . . . . Throw beams of light / from your dazzling throne . . . . / Get out of bed—you've slept long enough! / Come on the run before it's too late. / God, come back! / Smile your blessing smile: / *That* will be our salvation." (Ps 80:1–3, TM)

## Jeremiah

**Scripture**: "Now the word of the LORD came to me [, Jeremiah, ] saying, 'Before I formed you in the womb I knew you, / and before you were born I consecrated you; / I appointed you a prophet to the nations.' / Then I said, 'Ah, Lord GOD! Truly I do not know how to speak, for I am only a boy.' But the LORD said to me, 'Do not say, "I am only a boy," / for you shall go to all to whom I send you, / and you shall speak whatever I command you.'" (Jer 1:4–7, NRSVue)

**Reflection**: Jeremiah the prophet has a book of fifty-two chapters in the Bible named after him. As the above Scripture passage notes, the prophet's call predates his birth, as does his divine consecration. Even though he thought of himself as only a boy, the LORD considered him to be a manly prophet, who spoke during the reigns of Judah's last kings: Josiah (640–609 BCE), Jehoahaz (609 BCE), Jehoiakim (609–598 BCE), Jehoichin (598–597 BCE), and Zedekiah (597–586 BCE). Jeremiah's basic message was God's judgment on Judah for its idolatry and unfaithfulness with a call for repentance and a promise of future restoration. For example, the LORD sent him to prophesy in front of the LORD's house in Jerusalem: "Thus says the LORD of hosts, the God of Israel: I am now bringing upon this city and upon all its towns all the disaster that I have pronounced against it, because they have stiffened their necks, refusing to hear my words" (Jer 19:15, NRSVue). The chief officer in the house of the LORD—Pashhur—struck Jeremiah for what he said and, then, put him in the stocks (Jer 20:1–2). After spending the night in the stocks, Jeremiah was released the next morning. Jeremiah told him, "The LORD has named you not Pashhur but 'Terror-all-around.' For thus says the LORD: I am making you a terror to yourself and to all your friends, and they shall fall by the sword of their enemies while you look on. And I will give all Judah into the hand of the king of Babylon; he shall carry them captive to Babylon and shall kill them with the sword. And you, Pashhur, and all who live in your house, shall go into captivity, and to Babylon you shall go; there you shall die, and there you shall be buried, you and all your friends, to whom you have prophesied falsely" (Jer 20:3–4, 6, NRSVue). It is not difficult to understand that Jeremiah's mission of prophesying the destruction of Jerusalem upset many officials, not to mention the citizens. Nevertheless, his words came true when King Nebuchadnezzar of Babylon captured Jerusalem in 598 BCE and took King Jehoichin and all the royal household as captives to Babylon; then, he established King Zedekiah (597–586 BCE), Jehoichin's great-uncle, as a client king owing yearly tribute to Nebuchadnezzar. After Zedekiah revolted, Nebuchadnezzar returned to Jerusalem, destroyed the Temple, demolished the city walls, and took every able-bodied man, woman, and child with him as captives to Babylon in 586/587 BCE. Thus, the words of the prophet Jeremiah came true.

**Meditation/Journal**: In your life, who has been a prophet of destruction? Explain.

**Psalm Response**: "Alongside Babylon's rivers / we sat on the banks; we cried and cried, / remembering the good old days in [Jerusalem]. / Alongside the quaking aspens / we stacked our unplayed harps; / That's where our captors demanded songs, / sarcastic and mocking: / 'Sing us a happy [Jerusalem] song!' / Oh, how could we ever sing GOD's song / in this wasteland? / If I ever forgot you, Jerusalem, / let my fingers wither and fall off like leaves. / Let my tongue swell and turn black / if I fail to remember you, / If I fail, O dear Jerusalem, / to honor you as my greatest." (Ps 137:1–6, TM)

## Jesus

**Scripture**: ". . . [Jesus] took the twelve aside and said to them, 'Look, we are going up to Jerusalem, and everything that is written about the Son of Man by the prophets will be accomplished. For he will be handed over to the gentiles, and he will be mocked and insulted and spat upon. After they have flogged him, they will kill him, and on the third day he will rise again.'" (Luke 18:31–33, NRSVue)

**Reflection**: Among the author of Luke's Gospel's many views of who Jesus of Nazareth was is great prophet. As seen in the above Scripture passage, the Lukan Jesus predicts his own death and resurrection. That prediction is acknowledged as fulfilled by the two people on their way to Emmaus. When asked by the unrecognizable Jesus about what they are discussing, they tell him, "The things about Jesus of Nazareth, who was a prophet mighty in deed and word before God and all the people, and how our chief priests and leaders handed him over to be condemned to death and crucified him. Yes, and besides all this, it is now the third day since these things took place. Moreover, some women of our group astounded us. They were at the tomb early this morning, and when they did not find his body there they came back and told us that they had indeed seen a vision of angels who said that he was alive" (Luke 24:19b–20, 21b–23, NRSVue). While there are other predictions similar to the one in the above Scripture text (Luke 9:21, 44; 13:33), the Scripture passage above has been copied from Mark's Gospel (10:32–34) and further expanded by the author of Luke's Gospel, especially the words written by the prophets. Likewise, Luke 9:21 is found in Mark 8:31; Luke 9:44 is a shortened version of Mark 9:31; Luke 13:33 about it being "impossible for a prophet to be killed outside of Jerusalem" is unique to Luke's Gospel.

The author's perspective that Jesus was a prophet is scattered throughout Luke's Gospel. In the unique speech in the synagogue in Nazareth on the Sabbath, Jesus reads from the scroll of the prophet Isaiah (61:1–2) announcing that the words are fulfilled in him (Luke 4:16–23); that speech concludes with his words: "Truly I tell you, no prophet is accepted in his home town" (Luke 4:24) before the crowd drives him out of town (Luke 4:29). After witnessing the raising of the widow of Nain's son by Jesus—a story unique to Luke's Gospel—the crowd declares that a great prophet had arisen among them (Luke 7:16). Later, Jesus' disciples report that the crowds think that he is one of the ancient prophets who has arisen (Luke 9:19). Also, Luke emphasizes Jesus' prophetic knowledge, presenting him as knowing the thoughts of others (Luke 5:22; 7:39; 11:17). In the sermon on the plain (Luke 6:17), Jesus is characterized as being a prophet like Moses (Deut 18:15). The two men in Jesus' tomb tell the women visitors: "'[Jesus] is not here but has risen. Remember how he told you, while he was still in Galilee, that the Son of Man must be handed over to the hands of sinners and be crucified and on the third day rise again.' Then they remembered his words . . ." (Luke 24:5b–7, NRSVue). Thus, the Lukan Jesus is presented as a prophet, fulfilling the role of a divine messenger who speaks God's truth to people.

**Meditation/Journal**: Whom do you consider to be a prophet like Jesus? Explain.

**Psalm Response**: "Keep me safe, O God, / I've run for dear life to you. / I say to GOD, 'Be my Lord!' / Without you, nothing makes sense. / And these God-chosen lives all around— / what splendid friends they make! / Don't just go shopping for a god, / Gods are not for sale. / I swear I'll never treat god-names

/ like brand-names. / My choice is you, GOD, first and only. / And now I find I'm *your* choice!" (Ps 16:1–5, TM)

## Jezebel

**Scripture**: The Son of Man said to John of Patmos: ". . . [T]o the angel of the church in Thyatira write: . . . I have this against you: you tolerate that woman Jezebel, who calls herself a prophet and is teaching and beguiling my servants to engage in sexual immorality and to eat food sacrificed to idols. I gave her time to repent, but she refuses to repent of her sexual immorality." (Rev 2:18, 20–21, NRSVue)

**Reflection**: This false prophetess named Jezebel is not the same Jezebel, queen and wife of King Ahab of Israel (874–853 BCE) (1 Kgs 18:1–22:40); that Canaanite Queen Jezebel was responsible for the prophets and worship of Baal. The prophetess Jezebel in the CB (NT) book of Revelation represents John of Patmos' opponent. The Jezebel in the CB (NT) book of Revelation is fostering religious infidelity and idolatry in the trading center in Thyatira; the church there is at fault for tolerating the presence of "that woman Jezebel." The author of Revelation took the radical stance that there could be no compromise. The question was simple: To what extent could members of the church in Thyatira conform to the culture for the sake of economic survival? The author answers the question by telling the members of the church in Thyatira that they are to hold fast (Rev 2:25). There is no room for compromise.

**Meditation/Journal**: What is a recent economic compromise that the author of the CB (NT) book of Revelation would label a Jezebel?

**Psalm Response**: "Our God is in heaven / doing whatever he wants to do. / [The nations'] gods are metal and wood, / handmade in a basement shop: / Carved mouths that can't talk, / painted eyes that can't see, / Tin ears that can't hear, / molded noses that can't smell, / Hands that can't grasp, feet that can't walk or run, / throats that never utter a sound. / Those who make them have become just like them, / have become just like the gods they trust." (Ps 115:3–8, TM)

## Job

**Scripture**: Job said: ". . . I know that my vindicator lives / and that in the end he will stand upon the earth; / and after my skin has been destroyed, then in my flesh I shall see God, / whom I shall see on my side, / and my eyes shall behold, and not another. / My heart faints within me!" (Job 19:25–27, NRSVue)

**Reflection**: When reading the HB (OT) book of Job, it is important to know that a vindicator (redeemer) was usually a relative, who had the responsibility of ensuring the integrity of the family and its possessions. It was the redeemer's responsibility to reclaim anything that had been lost in, for example, bankruptcy or enslavement. That is the liberator that Job proclaims; in spite of all the rejection he experiences in the book, he perseveres, holding on to his own integrity, prophesying that one day he will see God either before or after he dies. Job's prophecy comes true when the LORD answered him out of the whirlwind (Job 38:1). Near the end of the book, Job tells God, "I had heard of you by the hearing of the ear, / but now my eye sees you" (Job 42:5). Job's vindicator or redeemer lives, and Job has seen him. This makes Job a true prophet.

**Meditation/Journal**: In your life, who has been your vindicator or redeemer? Explain.

**Psalm Response**: "I bless GOD every chance I get; / my lungs expand with his praise. / When I was desperate, I called out, / and GOD got me out of a tight spot. / Open your mouth and taste, open your eyes and see— / how good GOD is. / Blessed are you who run to him. / GOD keeps an eye on his friends, / his ears pick up every moan and groan. / Is anyone crying for help? GOD is listening, / ready to rescue you." (Ps 34:1, 6, 8, 15, 17, TM)

## Joel

**Scripture**: Peter said: ". . . [T]his is what was spoken through the prophet Joel: 'In the last days it will be, God declares, / that I will pour out my Spirit upon all flesh, / and your sons and your daughters shall prophesy, / and your young men shall see visions, / and your old men shall dream dreams. / Even upon my slaves, both men and women, / in those days I will pour out my Spirit, / and they shall prophesy.'" (Acts 2:16–18, NRSVue)

**Reflection**: In Peter's post-Pentecost speech in the CB (NT) Acts of the Apostles, he quotes from Joel (2:28–29), whom he identifies as a prophet (Acts 2:16). It is important to note here that the HB (OT) book of Joel does not refer to Joel as a prophet! Joel's words, written after the Babylonian captivity, stated that the prophetic gift of the spirit would be given to all people. The author of the Acts of the Apostles presents Peter interpreting the wind and fire of Pentecost (Acts 2:1–4) as the fulfillment of Joel's prophecy. God's Spirit poured out on many people signified the renewal of prophecy among all men and women: sons, daughters, young men, old men, and both male and female slaves. From the perspective of the author of the Acts of the Apostles, Joel's words came true; thus, he is a true prophet.

**Meditation/Journal**: In what specific ways have you experienced God's Spirit being poured on you? Or in what specific ways have you experienced God's Spirit being poured on one of your family members?

## John (of Patmos)

**Scripture**: "The revelation of Jesus Christ, which God gave [John] to show his servants what must soon take place, and he made it known by sending his angel to his servant John, who testified to the word of God and to the testimony of Jesus Christ, even to all that he saw. Blessed is the one who reads the words of the prophecy, and blessed are those who hear and who keep what is written in it, for the time is near." (Rev 1:1–3, NRSVue)

**Reflection**: First, the author of the CB (NT) book of Revelation thinks (believes) that he is writing prophecy. Second, since the prophecy comes from God through Jesus Christ, it is delivered by an angel to John on the island of Patmos (Rev 1:9); John "was in the spirit on the Lord's day" (Rev 1:10, NRSVue) when he hears a loud voice tell him to write what he saw (Rev 1:11). This makes John a prophet; he bears witness that he received the word of God and the testimony of Jesus Christ. Third, the prophecy is meant to be read by those who can read and to be heard by those who cannot read. In either case, they are to keep what they read or hear, because, as John thinks, the time of crisis or persecution is just about over. Fourth, the message from God is also a known letter from a prophet exiled on Patmos (Rev 1:9). While in popular understanding, apocalypse refers to disasters and destruction, in the biblical world of the first century CE, it meant to uncover, to reveal, to make something fully known. The meaning of events in a human life is, usually, hidden from people, but a vision from a world beyond this one can reveal the true meaning of history. Thus, a follower of Jesus gets to see behind the scenes to understand that the real meaning of life—its struggles and joys—is all about whether one follows the way of the world or the way of Jesus. In other words, the author of Revelation's view is that history is a contest between good and evil, the good guys dressed in white and the bad guys dressed in black, and everyone must, ultimately, choose sides.

**Meditation/Journal**: In what recent TV show, film, or book did you find a contest between good and evil? What was the good to be achieved? What was the evil to be avoided.

**Canticle Response**: "Salvation to our God on his Throne! / Salvation to the Lamb! / Oh, Yes! / The blessing and glory and wisdom and thanksgiving, / The honor and power and strength, / To our God forever and ever and ever! / Oh, Yes! / (Rev 7:10, 12, TM)

## John the Baptist

**Scripture**: "When John [the Baptist]'s messengers had gone, Jesus began to speak to the crowds about John: 'What . . . did you go out to see? A prophet? Yes, I tell you, and more than a prophet. This is the one about whom it is written, "See I am sending my messenger ahead of you, / who will prepare your way before you."'" (Luke 7:24, 26–27, NRSVue)

**Reflection**: In what is known by biblical scholars as Q (from *Quelle*, meaning *Source*), both the author of Matthew's Gospel (11:7–19) and the author of Luke's Gospel (7:24–35) present a scene of John the Baptist sending his followers to question Jesus, who refers to John as a prophet. The prophecy which John is understood to fulfill is taken from the HB (OT) prophet Malachi (3:1); however, it is only the first line of Malachi's words; the source used by the author of Matthew's Gospel and the author of Luke's Gospel adds "who will prepare your way before you," which does not appear in Malachi. In other words, the author of the Source (Q) has changed what Malachi wrote to make it fit the understood role of John the Baptist. The author of Luke's Gospel goes one step farther in declaring John the Baptist to be a prophet. On the day of John's circumcision, John's father, Zechariah, declares that he "will be called the / prophet of the Most High, / for [he] will go before the Lord to prepare his ways" (Luke 1:76, NRSVue). Thus, the Lukan Jesus' declaration that John the Baptist is a prophet reinforces John's father's declaration of the same, even using the words attributed to Malachi—to prepare the way of the Lord—which do not appear in Malachi!

**Meditation/Journal**: In your family, what words (or saying) are (is) attributed to an ancestor who, probably, never spoke those words?

**Canticle Response**: ". . . [Y]ou, my child [, John the Baptist], 'Prophet of the Highest,' / will go ahead of the Master to prepare his ways, / Present the offer of salvation to his people, / the forgiveness of their sins. / Through the heartfelt mercies of our God, / God's Sunrise will break in upon us, / Shining on those in the darkness, / those sitting in the shadow of death, / Then showing us the way, one foot at a time, / down the path of peace." (Luke 1:76–79, TM)

## Jonah

**Scripture**: "[King Jeroboam II of Israel (782–753 BCE)] restored the border of Israel . . . , according to the word of the LORD, the God of Israel, which he spoke by his servant Jonah . . . , the prophet . . . ." (2 Kgs 14:25)

**Reflection**: The "word of the LORD" indicated in the above Scripture passage spoken by the prophet Jonah is not recorded in biblical literature. The HB (OT) book of Jonah is a story about the word of the LORD coming to Jonah and sending him to Nineveh, the capital of Assyria, which captured the Northern Kingdom of Israel in 722 BCE. Thus, there is the irony that an Israelite prophet is sent to Israel's enemy's capital—Nineveh, Assyria—with the message to repent, which, again ironically, the king and all the people do (Jonah 3:6–10)! In the CB (NT), the author of Luke's Gospel presents Jonah as a prophetic sign of repentance (Luke 11:29–32), while the author of Matthew's Gospel presents him as a prophetic sign of the three days and nights that Jesus will spend in the tomb (Matt 12:39–41), just like Jonah was in the belly of a large fish for three days and three nights (Jonah 1:17).

**Meditation/Journal**: After reading the Canticle Response below, make a list of all the interpretations of the prophet Jonah presented above and below. What do you discover?

**Canticle Response**: "In trouble, deep trouble, I prayed to GOD. / He answered me. / From the belly of the grave I cried, 'Help!' / You heard my cry. / You threw me into ocean's depths, / into a watery grave, / With ocean waves, ocean breakers / crashing over me. / Yet you pulled me up from that grave alive, / O GOD, my God! / When my life was slipping away, / I remembered GOD, / And my prayer got through to you, / made it all the way to your Holy Temple." (Jonah 2:2–3, 6–7, TM)

## Joseph (son of Jacob)

**Scripture**: "[Joseph] said to [his eleven brothers:] 'Listen to this dream that I dreamed. There we were, binding sheaves in the field. Suddenly my sheaf rose and stood upright; then your sheaves gathered around it and bowed down to my sheaf.' His brothers said to him, 'Are you indeed to reign over us? Are you indeed to have dominion over us?' He had another dream and told it to his brothers, saying, 'Look, I have had another dream; the sun, the moon, and eleven stars were bowing down to me.'" (Gen 37:6–8ab; 9, NRSVue)

**Reflection**: Joseph, the eleventh son of the patriarch Jacob, is considered a prophet because his dreams, which are considered divine windows opening to the future, come true. The story about Joseph is the longest, continuous narrative in the HB (OT) book of Genesis (37:1—50:26). It is constructed around a series of three dream sequences; each sequence contains a pair of dreams (Gen 37:5–11; 40:5–23; 41:1–36). The focus here is on the pair of dreams in the Scripture passage above. After Joseph's brothers sell him into Egypt as a slave, he rises through the ranks to become second in command to Pharaoh—all because he can both tell Pharoah what he dreamed and interpret the meaning of the dream. The above Scripture passage is fulfilled when the Egyptian drought becomes a reality and Joseph's brothers go to Egypt to buy food. After they arrive, "Joseph's brothers came and bowed themselves before him, with their faces to the ground" (Gen 42:6b); the brothers do not recognize Joseph. Upon a second trip to buy more food, they "bowed to the ground before [Joseph]" (Gen 43:26). In other words, Joseph's first two divine dreams are fulfilled two times by his brothers. Thus, Joseph is considered a prophet.

**Meditation/Journal**: What dream have you recently dreamed that came true?

**Canticle Response**: "Joseph is a wild donkey, / a wild donkey by a spring, / spirited donkeys on a hill. / The archers with malice attacked, / shooting their hate-tipped arrows; / But he held steady under fire, / his bow firm, his arms limber, / With the backing of the Champion of Jacob, / the Shepherd, the Rock of Israel, / The God of your father—may he help you! / And may The Strong God—may he give you his blessings, / Blessings tumbling out of the skies, / blessings bursting up from the Earth— / blessings of breasts and womb. / May the blessings of your father / exceed the blessings of the ancient mountains, / surpass the delights of the eternal hills; / May they rest on the head of Joseph, / on the brow of the one consecrated among his brothers." (Gen 49:22–26, TM)

## Joseph (foster father of Jesus)

**Scripture**: ". . . [A]n angel of the Lord appeared to [Joseph] in a dream and said, 'Joseph, son of David, do not be afraid to take Mary as your wife, for the child conceived in her is from the Holy Spirit. She will bear a son, and you are to name him Jesus, for he will save his people from their sins.' All this took place to fulfill what had been spoken by the Lord through the prophet: 'Look, the virgin shall become pregnant and give birth to a son, / and they shall name him Emmanuel,' which means, 'God is with us.'" (Matt 1:20–23, NRSVue)

**Reflection**: There is little doubt among biblical scholars that the Joseph character presented in the CB (NT) gospel according to Matthew is modeled on the HB (OT) story of Joseph, son of Jacob, especially the motif of dreams serving as the revelation of divine plans. The Matthean Joseph is the son of Jacob (Matt 1:16) in the genealogy which begins the gospel (Matt 1:1–16). Once Mary's fiancée discovers her pregnancy, he decides to divorce her quietly (1:19) to avoid both of them being shamed. That's when God reveals his plan, according to the author, through Joseph's dream. The "angel of the Lord" is a HB (OT) code phrase for God, the LORD. The message he delivers is that Mary's pregnancy is divinely ordained (Holy Spirit); therefore, Joseph should abandon his plan and accept God's plan, which, according to this author, was predicted by the prophet Isaiah (7:14); however, Isaiah's words are addressed to King Ahaz of Judah (732–716 BCE), and they refer to "the young woman . . . with child [who] shall bear a son and shall name him Immanuel" (Isa 7:16, NRSVue), probably Ahaz's wife. Not only is the prophet Isaiah well known for giving children names that describe their function, but the child announced to Ahaz insures the Davidic line; he is most likely Hezekiah, who succeeded his father to Judah's throne. In its original context, the promise—"God with us"—in the person of Hezekiah, has nothing to do with Jesus, no matter what the author of Matthew's Gospel reinterprets it to mean! It was not until after the Davidic line of Judean kings was eliminated that the quotation from Isaiah began to take on messianic interpretation and expectation. The child's name, Immanuel, was meant to insure King Ahaz that God was his true helper; thus, he needed no alliance with any other nation to keep his enemies at bay. After the author of Matthew's Gospel presents the altered quotation from the prophet Isaiah, he proceeds to fulfill it with the birth of Jesus in Bethlehem of Judea, where his mother and foster father live (Matt 2:1). And, thus, according to prophetic understanding, Joseph, foster father of Jesus, is a prophet, like his HB (OT) namesake.

**Meditation/Journal**: In your family, whose (parent, uncle, aunt, etc.) reinterpreted words are used in a modern context to refer to something, to which they did not originally apply? Explain.

**Psalm Response**: "God, God . . . my God! / . . . [Y]ou were midwife at my birth, / setting me at my mother's breasts! / When I left the womb you cradled me; / since the moment of birth you've been my God. / Our children and their children / will get in on this / As the word is passed along / from parent to child. / Babies not yet conceived / will hear the good news— / that God does what he says." (Ps 22:1a, 9–10, 30–31, TM)

## Joshua

**Scriptures**: The LORD said to Moses, "Joshua son of Nun, your assistant, shall enter [the promised land]; encourage him, for he is the one who will secure Israel's possession of it." (Deut 1:38, NRSVue)

". . . Moses summoned Joshua and said to him in the sight of all Israel: 'Be strong and bold, for you are the one who will go with this people into the land that the LORD has sworn to their ancestors to give them; and you will put them in possession of it. It is the LORD who goes before you. He will be with you; he will not fail you or forsake you. Do not fear or be dismayed.'" (Deut 31:7–8, NRSVue)

"The LORD said to Moses, 'Your time to die is near; call Joshua and present yourselves in the tent of meeting, so that I may commission him.' So Moses and Joshua went and presented themselves in the tent of meeting, and the LORD appeared at the tent in a pillar of cloud; the pillar of cloud stood at the entrance to the tent." (Deut 31:14–15, NRSVue)

"Then the LORD commissioned Joshua son of Nun and said, 'Be strong and bold for you shall bring the Israelites into the land that I promised them; I will be with you.'" (Deut 31:23, NRSVue)

"Joshua son of Nun was full of the spirit of wisdom, because Moses had laid his hands on him; and the Israelites obeyed him, doing as the LORD had commanded Moses." (Deut 34:9, NRSVue)

**Reflection**: From the very first chapter of the HB (OT) book of Deuteronomy, Joshua is described as Moses' successor. His primary responsibility, as can be deduced from the Scriptures above, is to lead the Israelites across the Jordan River into the land God promised to give Abraham, Isaac, and Jacob and their descendants: the newly escaped Hebrews from Egyptian slavery. The HB (OT) book of Joshua continues the story, stating: "After the death of Moses the servant of the LORD, the LORD spoke to Joshua son of Nun, Moses' assistant, saying, 'My servant Moses is dead. Now proceed to cross the Jordan, you and all this people, into the land that I am giving to them, to the Israelites'" (Josh 1:1–2, NRSVue). Then, after some preparation, the Israelites form a grand procession crossing the Jordan (Josh 3:1—4:24) under the leadership of Joshua, of whom Moses would have been proud. Joshua is considered a prophet because he receives direct divine instructions about leading the Israelites across the Jordan River. His role is the culmination of the LORD's prophecies to Abraham and Moses. Furthermore, he is the recipient of direct divine communication, like Moses; he is a mini-Moses character, a prophetic conduit for God's word and will to the Israelites.

**Meditation/Journal**: Who in your family is a mini-version of an ancestor? Explain.

**Song Response**: "Listen, Heavens, I have something to tell you. / Attention, Earth, I've got a mouth full of words. / My teaching, let it fall like a gentle rain, / my words arrive like morning dew, / Like a sprinkling rain on new grass, / like spring showers on the garden. / For it's GOD's Name I'm preaching— / respond to the greatness of our God! / The Rock: His works are perfect, / and the way he works is fair and just; / A God you can depend upon, no exceptions, / a straight-arrow God." (Deut 32:1–4, TM)

## Jotham

**Scripture**: "The trees once went out / to anoint a king over themselves. / So they said to the olive tree, / 'Reign over us.' / The olive tree answered them, / 'Shall I stop producing my rich oil / by which gods and mortals are honored / and go to sway over the trees?' / Then the trees said to the fig tree, / 'You come and reign over us.' / But the fig tree answered them, / 'Shall I stop producing my sweetness / and my delicious fruit / and go to sway over the trees?' / Then the trees said to the vine, / 'You come and reign over us.' / But the vine said to them, 'Shall I stop producing my wine / that cheers gods and mortals / and go to sway over the trees?' / So all the trees said to the bramble, / 'You come and reign over us.' / And the bramble said to the trees, / 'If in good faith you are anointing me king over you, / then come and take refuge in my shade, / but if not, let fire come out of the bramble / and devour the cedars of Lebanon.'" (Judg 8:8–15, NRSVue)

**Reflection**: Following Jerubbaal's (Gideon's) success as a judge (Judg 6:11—8:35), Abimelech, born of a concubine and one of Jerubbaal's seventy-one sons, goes to his father's house and kills seventy of his brothers. Then, Abimelech is made king by the lords of Shechem. Jotham, another of Jerubbaal's sons, escapes Abimelech's slaughter. After Abimelech is crowned king, Jotham ascends a mountain and tells the lords of Shechem the above Scripture, commonly labeled the parable of the trees; however, it is best understood as an allegory or a fable. In the allegory, Abimelech is the bramble or thorny bush; he is unworthy and self-serving and brings destruction upon those who chose him to be king (Judg 9:22–57). His reign is marked by conflict, violence, and ultimately his death at the hands of a woman, who dropped a millstone on his head, fulfilling Jotham's prophecy (Judg 9:53). In the parable, the trees are arranged in the order of perceived significance. The olive tree provided food and oil for anointings of prophets, priests, and kings. The fig tree provided food and shade. The vine produced grapes from which wine was made for drinking and, once the vine had grown for years, it could provide shade. However, the bramble or thorny bush was useless; its presence in the story brings a negative into play. Abimelech is a thorny character, who, after the olive, fig, and vine refuse kingship—according to Jotham—is crowned king under an oak tree (Judg 9:6)!

**Meditation/Journal**: Besides the application of the parable, analogy, or fable above, what other application might the parable, analogy, or fable have for you? Explain.

**Psalm Response**: "God will tear you limb from limb, / sweep you up and throw you out, / Pull you up by the roots / from the land of life. / Good people will watch and / worship. They'll laugh in relief: / 'Big Man bet on the wrong horse, / trusted in big money, / made his living from catastrophe.' / And I'm an olive tree, / growing green in God's house. / I trusted in the generous mercy / of God then and now. / I thank you always / that you went into action." (Ps 52:5–9a, TM)

## Judas Barsabbas

**Scripture**: ". . . [T]he apostles and the elders, with the consent of the whole church, . . . sent Judas called Barsabbas . . . with the . . . letter. Judas . . . , who [was himself a prophet], said much to encourage and strengthen the brothers and sisters [of gentile origin in Antioch and Syria and Cilicia]. After [he] had been there for some time, [he was] sent off in peace by the brothers and sisters to those who had sent [him]." (Acts 15:22–23a, 32–33)

**Reflection**: Like many other prophets, who make only one or two appearances in biblical literature, Judas called Barsabbas appears only in chapter 15 of the CB (NT) Acts of the Apostles. Along with a fellow prophet, he is sent with a letter containing the results of the council held in Jerusalem. The issues that precipitated the gathering of apostles and elders in Jerusalem concerned the circumcision of gentile men, dietary regulations, and sexual immorality (Acts 15:23–29). With the letter, Judas travelled to Antioch, where he delivered the letter to the believers. Then, after a while, the community sent him back to Jerusalem, and that is the last he is heard of in the CB (NT). His name—Barsabbas—can mean *son of Sabbas* (his father's name) or *son of the Sabbath*—indicating that he was born on the Sabbath. The author of the CB (NT) Acts of the Apostles identifies him as a prophet, which means that he had the ability to speak messages given by God through the Spirit. The name Judah means *praise or thanksgiving;* it carries the connotation of moral integrity and adherence to what is right. Thus, the author of the Acts of the Apostles applies a name to the person bearing a letter that emphasizes the qualities of righteousness and impartiality—exactly what the gentiles were hoping to hear from the Jews.

**Meditation/Journal**: In your life, who could bear the name Judas because he or she is just, fair, or upright? Explain.

**Psalm Response**: "Hallelujah! / I give thanks to GOD with everything I've got— / Wherever good people gather, and in the congregation. / GOD's works are so great, worth / A lifetime of study—endless enjoyment! / Splendor and beauty mark his craft; / His generosity never gives out. / He manufactures truth and justice; / All his products are guaranteed to last— / Never out-of-date, never obsolete, rust-proof." (Ps 111:1–3, 7–8, TM)

# 5

# K–N

## FROM KING NEBUCHADNEZZAR TO NOAH

### King Nebuchadnezzar

**Scripture**: ". . . Nebuchadnezzar dreamed such dreams that his spirit was troubled and his sleep left him. So the king commanded that the magicians, the enchanters, the sorcerers, and the Chaldeans be summoned to tell the king his dreams. The king answered the Chaldeans, 'This is a public decree: if you do not tell me both the dream and its interpretation, you shall be torn limb from limb, and your houses shall be laid in ruins.'" (Dan 2:1–2, 5, NRSVue)

**Reflection**: Nebuchadnezzar II was the second king of Babylon from 605 to 562 BCE. While in Judaism he is not generally considered a prophet, in Christianity he is sometimes considered a prophet because he experiences prophetic dreams needing an interpretation by Daniel in the HB (OT) book of Daniel. After having a dream that troubled him greatly, the king sought help from those in Babylon who were recognized as interpreters, but they could not interpret what the king would not tell them (Dan 2:7–11). The king's rationale was that they tell him what he dreamed so he could check the reliability of their interpretation. Because they are unable to do so, the stage is set for Daniel, a young, captive Jew, to enter the scene by way of prayer (contrasted to magic) and to receive from God in a vision (not a dream) of the night (Dan 2:19) Nebuchadnezzar's dream, thus demonstrating the futility of Babylonian divination! Then, Daniel both tells the king his dream and interprets it for him (Dan 2:31–45).

**Meditation/Journal**: With whom have you shared one of your dreams? How did he or she help you interpret it?

**Prayer Response**: "Blessed be the name of God, / forever and ever. / He knows all, does all: / He changes the seasons and guides history, / He raises up kings and also brings them down, / he provides both intelligence and discernment, / He opens up the depths, tells secrets, / sees in the dark—light spills out of him! / God of all my ancestors, all thanks! all praise! / You made me wise and strong, / And now you've shown us what we ask for. / You've solved the king's mystery." (Dan 2:19–23, TM)

## King Saul

**Scripture**: ". . . [A] band of prophets met [Saul], and the spirit of God possessed him, and he fell into a prophetic frenzy along with them. When all who knew him before saw how he prophesied with the prophets, the people said to one another, 'What has come over the son of Kish? Is Saul also among the prophets?'" (1 Sam 10:10–11, NRSVue)

**Reflection**: Samuel had already taken "a vial of oil and poured it on [Saul's] head and kissed him; [and] said, 'The LORD has anointed you ruler over his people Israel'" (1 Sam 10:1). Also, Samuel had told him that he would meet a band of prophets and the spirit of the LORD would possess him and he would enter into a prophetic frenzy along with them (1 Sam 10:5–6). Thus, the LORD's spirit empowers Saul both to rule and to prophesy. The author of this narrative discloses some information about the phenomenon of prophecy in Israel. While most of the time Bible readers think of prophets as sole individuals with a spoken and/or written message, the author of the HB (OT) book of First Samuel reveals that there were groups of prophets in ancient Israel. This group is not responsible for speaking a message or writing a book, but only to enter into an ecstatic trance, partially stimulated by music (1 Sam 10:5). On his way home, Saul enters into their state of spiritual or divine inspiration; such divine empowerment with the band of prophets confirms God's choice of Saul as the first king of Israel (1 Sam 1:5–6). In answer to the last question—"Is Saul also among the prophets?"—the answer is Yes.

**Meditation/Journal**: When have you experienced a state of spiritual or divine inspiration as a member of a group? What did it confirm for you?

**Psalm Response**: "If you [, GOD,] wake me each morning with the sound of your loving voice, / I'll go to sleep each night trusting in you. / Point out the road I must travel; / I'm all ears, all eyes before you. / Teach me how to live to please you, / because you're my God. / Lead me by your blessed Spirit / into cleared and level pastureland." (Ps 143:8, 10, TM)

## King Solomon

**Scripture**: ". . . [T]he LORD appeared to Solomon in a dream by night, and God said, 'Ask what I should give you.' And Solomon said, 'Give your servant . . . an understanding mind to govern your people, able to discern between good and evil . . . .' It pleased the LORD that Solomon had asked this. God said to him, 'I now do according to your word. Indeed, I give you a wise and discerning mind; no one like you has been before you, and no one like you shall arise after you.'" (1 Kgs 3:5, 9, 12, NRSVue)

**Reflection**: While not always considered a prophet, Solomon, King of all Israel (970–930 BCE), fills the prophetic role through the wisdom he requested and received from God. He is not designated a prophet in biblical literature, but his wisdom and divine inspiration behind it can be understood as prophetic qualities. Solomon asked God for an understanding mind so that he could govern or judge the people of Israel, and the LORD granted his request. He sought divine revelation through his petition in a dream. His request resulted in holy wisdom, which made him unique among the royalty which followed him in both Judah and Israel.

**Meditation/Journal**: Whom do you know who has a reputation for his or her wisdom? Explain.

**Psalm Response**: "Generous in love—God, give grace! / Huge in mercy—wipe out my bad record. / You have all the facts before you; / whatever you decide about me is fair. / I've been out of step with you for a long time, / in the wrong since before I was born. / What you're after is truth from the inside out. / Enter me, then; conceive a new, true life." (Ps 51:1, 4–6, TM)

## Lucius of Cyrene

**Scripture**: ". . . [I]n the church at Antioch there were prophets and teachers: . . . Lucius of Cyrene . . . . While they were worshiping the Lord and fasting, the

Holy Spirit said, 'Set apart for me Barnabas and Saul for the work to which I have called them.' Then after fasting and praying they laid their hands on them and sent them off." (Acts 13:1–3, NRSVue)

**Reflection**: Biblically, the only place where the prophet Lucius of Cyrene is mentioned is in the passage above from the CB (NT) Acts of the Apostles. The author presents him as one of several-named founders of the church in Antioch. While he is not named, he may have been among those who traveled from Jerusalem to Antioch or from Cyrene to Antioch (Acts 11:19–20). Another Lucius is mentioned in Paul's letter to the Romans (16:21), but there is no way to tell if it is the same man. And, finally, in history Lucius was occasionally identified with Luke, the author of Luke-Acts. Thus, what is known about Lucius of Cyrene is ambiguous, because he is otherwise unknown. All the author of the Acts of the Apostles tells the reader is that the group of prophets and teachers in Antioch were fasting in preparation for a divine revelation, which they received. Then, being obedient to the Holy Spirit and after laying their hands in blessing on Barnabas and Saul, the prophets and teachers sent them on their journey (Acts 13:4–6).

**Meditation/Journal**: Who are the members of your extended family that you know nothing about?

**Psalm Response**: "Listen, GOD! Please, pay attention! / Can you make sense of these ramblings, / my groans and cries? / King-God, I need your help. / Every morning / you'll hear me at it again. / Every morning / I lay out the pieces of my life / on your altar / and watch for fire to descend. / . . . [H]ere I am . . . / Waiting for directions . . . ." (Ps 5:1–3, 7a, 8a, TM)

## Malachi

**Scripture**: "An oracle. The word of the LORD to Israel by Malachi. 'I have loved you,' says the LORD." (Mal 1:1–2a, NRSVue)

**Reflection**: In the HB (OT), the book of the prophet Malachi consists of four chapters. The name—Malachi—means *my messenger*. Thus, the name can be that of an individual or a title for the author of the short, post-exilic, prophetic book. The author of the book emphasizes his concern about a lack of serious devotion on the part of the Babylonian exiles (Jews), who have returned to Judah's rebuilt temple. At the beginning of chapter 3, there is a promise from the LORD to send his messenger to prepare the way for his coming (Mal 3:1); he is called the "messenger of the covenant" (Mal 3:1, NRSVue). While the messenger is not identified, at the end of the book the LORD promises to send the prophet Elijah (Mal 4:5); the expectation of the return of Elijah is founded on the tradition that he did not die but was taken into heaven (2 Kgs 2:11). CB (NT) authors identify John the Baptist with Elijah (Mark 9:9–13; Matt 178:9–13; Luke 1:17), who appears with Jesus (and Moses) at his transfiguration (Mark 9:2–8; Matt 17:1–8; Luke 9:28–36).

**Meditation/Journal**: Who has been a messenger of good news to you?

**Psalm Response**: "GOD, my God, how great you are! / beautiful, gloriously robed, / Dressed up in sunshine, / and all heaven stretched out for your tent. / You built your palace on the ocean deeps, / made a chariot out of clouds and took off on wind-wings. / You commandeered winds as messengers, / appointed fire and flame as ambassadors." (Ps 104:1b–4, TM)

## Manaen

**Scripture**: ". . . [I]n the church at Antioch there were prophets and teachers: . . . Manaen, a childhood friend of Herod the ruler . . . . While they were worshiping the Lord and fasting, the Holy Spirit said, 'Set apart for me Barnabas and Saul for the work to which I have called them.' Then after fasting and praying they laid their hands on them and sent them off." (Acts 13:1–3, NRSVue)

**Reflection**: The prophetic Manaen (Menahem) is a leader in the church at Antioch, according to the Acts of the Apostles. However, he with two others—Simeon and Lucius—are unknown, except for the one reference in the CB (NT) Acts of the Apostles. Manaen is a former associate of Herod the tetrarch. The Greek word used to describe Manaen can mean foster-brother, nursed-together, reared-together, or educated-together. NRSV translates the Greek word as "a member of the court of Herod the ruler" (tetrarch), while, as can be seen in the above Scripture verse, NRSVue translates the Greek word as "a childhood friend of Herod the ruler," while TM states that he was "an advisor to the ruler Herod." No matter how the Greek word is translated, it remains a strange way to identify a prophetic teacher in the church at Antioch! Herod Antipas, son of Herod the Great, was born before 20 BCE, ruled Galilee and Perea from 4 BCE to 39 CE, and died after 39 CE. In CB (NT) literature, he is remembered primarily for the death of John the Baptist (Mark 6:14–29; Matt 14:1–12; Luke 9:7–9). Also, the author of Matthew's Gospel features him in the unique story about the visit of wise men and the death of children in Bethlehem (Matt 2:1–23), while the author of Luke's Gospel features Pilate sending Jesus to Herod during his trial before Pilate (Luke 23:6–12). To associate Manaen with Herod Antipas presents a negative vibe. Herod was cunning; he married Herodias, his brother's wife, which became the issue for the Baptist's death.

**Meditation/Journal**: Who is Manaen in your life, that is, someone associated with another who has a bad reputation? Explain.

**Psalm Response**: "Praise GOD, everybody! / Applaud GOD, all people! / His love has taken over our lives; / GOD's faithful ways are eternal. / Hallelujah!" (Ps 117:1–2, TM)

## Man of God

**Scripture**: "A man of God came out of Judah by the word of the LORD to Bethel, while Jeroboam was standing by the altar to offer incense. And he cried out against the altar by the word of the LORD and said, 'O altar, altar, thus says the LORD: A son shall be born to the house of David, Josiah by name, and he shall sacrifice on you the priests of the high places who offer incense on you . . . .' He gave a sign the same day, saying, 'This is the sign that the LORD has spoken: The altar shall be torn down, and the ashes that are on it shall be poured out.' When the king heard that the man of God cried out against the altar at Bethel, Jeroboam stretched out his hand from the altar . . . . But the hand that he stretched out against him withered so that he could not draw it back to himself. The altar was torn down, and the ashes poured out from the altar, according to the sign that the man of God had given by the word of the LORD. The king said to the man of God, 'Entreat now the favor of the LORD your God, and pray for me, so that my hand may be restored to me.' So the man of God entreated the LORD, and the king's hand was restored to him and became as it was before." (1 Kgs 13:1–6, NRSVue)

**Reflection**: This unnamed man of God is a prophet (1 Kgs 13:18) from the Southern Kingdom of Judah sent to Bethel, where one of Jeroboam's gold calves was located (1 Kgs 12:28–29), in the Northern Kingdom of Israel at the time of Jeroboam I (931–910 BCE). While the chronology is inaccurate—King Josiah of Judah (640–608 BCE) is credited with destroying the shrine in Bethel (2 Kgs 23:15–18), the man of God's sign that the altar would be torn down was fulfilled 300 hundred years later! Furthermore, within the story (legend) the man of God proves he is a prophet by restoring Jeroboam's withered hand, after Jeroboam asks him to do so. In other words, the prophecy of the restored hand is enacted, just like the destruction of the altar in Bethel was enacted by King Josiah 300 years later.

**Meditation/Journal**: In your family, what prediction (prophesy) made by an ancestor has been fulfilled?

**Psalm Response**: "God, it seems you've been our home forever; / long before the mountains were born, / Long before you brought earth itself to birth, / from 'once upon a time' to 'kingdom come'—you are God. / We live for seventy years or so / (with luck we might make it to eighty) . . . . / Oh! Teach us to live well! / Teach us to live wisely and well! / Let your servants see what you're best at— / the ways you rule and bless your children." (Ps 90:1–2, 10, 12, 16, TM)

## Mary (mother of Jesus)

**Scripture**: ". . . [T]he angel Gabriel was sent by God to a town in Galilee called Nazareth, to a virgin engaged to a man whose name was Joseph, of the house of David. The virgin's name was Mary. And he came to her and said, 'Greetings, favored one! The Lord is with you.' But she was much perplexed by his words and pondered what sort of greeting this might be. The angel said to her, 'Do not be afraid, Mary, for you have found favor with God. And now, you will conceive in your womb and bear a son, and you will name him Jesus.' Mary said to the angel, 'How can this be, since I am a virgin?' The angel said to her, 'The Holy Spirit will come upon you, and the power of the Most High will overshadow you; therefore the child to be born will be holy; he will be called Son of God. And now, your relative Elizabeth in her old age has also conceived a son, and this is the sixth month for her who was said to be barren.' Then Mary said, 'Here am I, the servant of the Lord; let it be with me according to your word.' Then the angel departed from her." (Luke 1:26–31, 34–36, 38, NRSVue)

**Reflection**: While there is no such scene as that depicted in the above passage from the CB (NT) in the gospels of Mark, Matthew, and John, the narrative with dialogue in Luke presents a call narrative experienced by many prophets. Following HB (OT) sources, the author of Luke's Gospel presents a pattern beginning with a divine encounter—some type of theophany or manifestation of God. In the above narrative that is the angel Gabriel, which means *God is Strong*. The second part of the pattern is an introductory word or greeting; Gabriel meets Mary and calls her God's graced one before telling her that the Lord is with her. This leads to the third part of the pattern: the objection. The narrator tells the reader that Mary is perplexed; in fact she tells Gabriel that it is impossible that she can conceive a child because she is a virgin. Nevertheless, Gabriel states that because she has been graced by God, she will conceive a child by the Holy Spirit and the overshadowing power of the Most High. The next part of the pattern, the sign, is Mary's relative Elizabeth, who was barren but in her old age has conceived a son. And the final part of the prophetic call pattern is Mary's acceptance of her pregnancy. Thus the unknown Mary of Nazareth becomes a prophetic spokesperson for God, invested with power, a message, and a mission in her own person or flesh. Her prophetic mission proclaims what God will do once her son is born (Luke 1:46–56).

In John's Gospel in the CB (NT), Mary functions as a prophetess in the wedding in Cana story (John 2:1–11). In that unique Johannine account, she indicates when it is time for Jesus to begin his public ministry. After telling her son that all the wine had been consumed, Jesus tells her that fact is no concern of his, as his hour had not come (John 2:3–4); *hour* indicates his divine manifestation. After ignoring his response, his mother tells the servants to do whatever he tells them (John 2:5). After filling water jars with water, they draw out wine, and, as a result of this first sign of Jesus, his disciples believe in him (John 2:6–11). Thus, is Mary, mother of Jesus, presented as a prophetess. She makes God and God's work the center of her life.

**Meditation/Journal**: Whom do you know who has made God and his work the center of his or her life? Explain how.

**Canticle Response**: "I'm bursting with God-news; / I'm dancing the song of my Savior God. / God took one good look at me, and look what happened— / I'm the most fortunate woman on earth! / What God has done for me will never be forgotten, / the God whose very name is holy, set apart from all others. / His mercy flows in wave after wave / on those who are in awe before him." (Luke 1:46–50, TM)

## Medad

**Scripture**: ". . . Moses . . . gathered seventy of the elders of the people . . . . Then the LORD came down in the cloud and spoke to him and took some of the spirit that was on him and put it on the seventy elders, and when the spirit rested upon them, they prophesied. Two men remained in the camp, one named . . . Medad, and the spirit rested on [him]; [he was] among those registered, but [he] had not gone out . . . , so [he] prophesied in the camp. And a young man ran and told Moses, '. . . Medad [is] prophesying in the camp.' And Joshua son of Nun, the assistant of Moses, one of his chosen men, said, 'My lord Moses, stop [him]!' But Moses said to him, 'Are you jealous for my sake? Would that all of the LORD's people were prophets and that the LORD would put his spirit on them!" (Num 11:24–25a, 26–29)

**Reflection**: The above Scripture text from the HB (OT) book of Numbers is the only biblical account concerning the prophet Medad. Not only is nothing else known about him, but the words of his prophecy are not recorded. He is one of seventy-two elders, who are chosen to help govern the Israelites. However, he did not go to the shared-spirit event, but he received some of the spirit of Moses, just like the other elders. After a tattle-tale young man informs Moses about the extra-spirit event, Joshua tells Moses to stop Medad from prophesying. In response, Moses expresses his wish that God would make all his people prophets by putting his spirit on them. This account of Medad's reception of the spirit is connected to the story following it about the quails. In Hebrew the word for breath, wind, and spirit is *ruah*. Thus, the *ruah* that prompts Medad to prophesy is the same *ruah* that goes out from the LORD and brings quails to the Israelite camp (Num 11:31). The breath, wind, and spirit of God cannot be controlled by human beings.

**Meditation/Journal**: What has been your most recent experience of being unable to control the breath, wind, or spirit? Explain.

**Psalm Response**: "[GOD,] Is there anyplace I can go to avoid your Spirit? / to be out of your sight? / If I climb to the sky, you're there! / If I go underground, you're there! / If I flew on morning's wings, / to the far western horizon, / You'd find me in a minute— / you're already there waiting! / Then I said to myself, 'Oh, he even sees me in the dark! / At night I'm immersed in the light!' / It's a fact: darkness isn't dark to you; / night and day, darkness and light, they're all the same to you." (Ps 139:7–12, TM)

## Micah

**Scripture**: "The word of the LORD that came to Micah . . . , which he saw concerning Samaria and Jerusalem. . . . / [T]he LORD is coming out of his place / and will come down and tread upon the high places of the earth. / . . . [T]his is for the transgression of Jacob / and for the sins of the house of Israel. / What is the transgression of Jacob? / Is it not Samaria? / And what is the high place of Judah? / Is it not Jerusalem? / Therefore I will make Samaria a heap in the open country . . . . / All her images shall be beaten to pieces . . . / and all her idols I will lay waste . . . / . . . [H]er wound is incurable. / It has come to Judah; / it has reached to the gate of my people, / to Jerusalem. / . . . [D]isaster has come down from the LORD / to the gate of Jerusalem." (Mic 1:1, 3, 5–6a, 7a, 9, 12b, NRSVue)

**Reflection**: The prophet Micah, comprised of seven chapters, occupies around six printed pages in most Bible. As can be seen in the above Scripture text, the prophet's focus is on Samaria, the capital of the Northern Kingdom of Israel, and Jerusalem, the capital of the Southern Kingdom of Judah. At the time he was writing, during the reigns of Judean King Jotham (740–732 BCE), King Ahaz (732–716 BCE), and King Hezekiah (716–687 BCE), both Jerusalem and Samaria were threatened by the expansion of the Assyrian empire. Basically, Micah declares that both capitals will fall. Samaria fell to the Assyrians in 722 BCE, during Micah's career as a prophet in the south. Nevertheless, Micah's words are delivered to rulers, who were both corrupt and complacent both in Samaria and Jerusalem. While Micah had long disappeared from the scene, Jerusalem fell to the Babylonians in 586/587 BCE. Micah's basic message is that idolatry and corruption will not be tolerated by the LORD.

**Meditation/Journal**: Whom do you hear proclaiming the same basic message as Micah?

**Response**: "How can I stand up before GOD / and show proper respect to the high God? / . . . [H]e's already made it plain how to live, what to do, / what GOD is looking for in men and women. / It's quite simple: Do what is fair and just to your neighbor, / be compassionate and loyal in your love, / and don't take yourself too seriously— / take God seriously. / Attention! GOD calls out to the city! / If you know what's good for you, you'll listen. / So listen all of you! / This is serious business." (Mic 6:6, 8–9, TM)

## Micaiah

**Scripture**: ". . . [T]he king of Israel [Ahab (874–853 BCE)] gathered the prophets together, . . . and said to them, 'Shall I go to battle . . . or shall I refrain?' They said, 'Go up, for the LORD will give [the town] into the hand of the king.' But Jehoshaphat [King of Judah (870–848 BCE) said, 'Is there no other prophet of the LORD here of whom we may inquire?' The king of Israel said to Jehoshaphat, 'There is still one other by whom we may inquire of the LORD, Micaiah . . . , but I hate him, for he never prophesies anything favorable about me but only disaster.' . . . Micaiah said, 'Therefore hear the word of the LORD: I saw the LORD sitting on his throne, with all the host of heaven standing beside him to the right and to the left of him. And the LORD said, "Who will entice Ahab, so that he may go up and fall . . .?" . . . [A] certain spirit came forward and stood before the LORD, saying, "I will entire him." "How?" the LORD asked him. He replied, "I will go out and be a lying spirit in the mouth of all his prophets."' Then Zedekiah . . . came up to Micaiah, slapped him on the cheek, and said, 'Which way did the spirit of the LORD pass from me to speak to you?' [During the battle] a certain man drew his bow and unknowingly struck the king of Israel between the scale armor and the breastplate . . . [and] at evening he died. So the king died and was brought to Samaria; they buried the king in Samaria." (1 Kgs 22:5b–8a, 19–20a, 21, 22ab, 24, 34–35, 37, NRSVue)

**Reflection**: The biblical story featuring the prophet Micaiah occupies chapter 22 of the First Book of Kings in the HB (OT) with a parallel account in Second Chronicles chapter 18. The story features dueling prophets. King Ahab of Israel gathers 400 prophets (1 Kgs 22:6), and all of them tell him the same thing: Go fight the battle; the LORD is on your side, and you will win. However, King Jehoshaphat of Judah, who is joining Ahab in battle, needs more assurance! So Ahab calls for Micaiah, who has been prompted to speak what the other 400 prophets have said. However, Micaiah disregards the prompt and, after describing his vision of the LORD, he says that a lying spirit has entered the other 400 prophets. Now, the prophetic battle is one against 400! In other words, when Micaiah is pressured to speak the truth, he delivers truth that no one wants to hear: Ahab will be killed in battle; Ahab orders him imprisoned. While fighting, Ahab is wounded and dies. Thus Micaiah's prophecy comes true.

**Meditation/Journal**: Whom have you known to stand up to a group with a message that is contradictory? What was the result?

**Psalm Response**: "I love GOD because he listened to me, / listened as I begged for mercy. / He listened so intently / as I laid out my case before him. 'Please, GOD!' I cried out. / 'Save my life!' / GOD is gracious—it is he who makes things right, / our most compassionate God. / I'm striding in the presence of GOD, / alive in the land of the living! / Despite giving up on the human race, / saying, 'They're all liars and cheats.'" (Ps 116:1–2, 4–5, 9, 11, TM)

## Miriam

**Scripture**: ". . . [T]he prophet[ess] Miriam, Aaron's sister, took a tambourine in her hand, and all the women went out after her with tambourines and with dancing. And Miriam sang to them: 'Sing to the LORD, for he has triumphed gloriously; / horse and rider he has thrown into the sea.'" (Exod 14:20–21, NRSVue)

**Reflection**: Miriam is presented as a prophetess by the author of the HB (OT) book of Exodus. She leads Israelite women in a victory song after the people escape from the Egyptian Pharaoh's army at the Sea of Reeds. Biblically, women usually sing victory songs after military success in ancient Israel. Long before that, however, after her brother, Moses, is born and hidden for three months (Exod 2:2), Miriam, standing on the river bank, watches the papyrus basket into which he was placed to see what would happen to him (Exod 2:4). Once he is rescued by Pharoah's daughter, she goes and gets the child's own mother to serve as his nurse (Exod 2:5–10). The HB (OT) book of Numbers indicates that she joined her brother, Aaron, in speaking against their brother, Moses (Num 12:1; 26:59). She and Aaron acknowledge that the LORD speaks through them (Num 12:2), which indicates that both of them are prophets. The LORD reminds them: "When there are prophets among you, / I the LORD make myself known to them in visions; / I speak to them in dreams. / Not so with my servant Moses . . . . / With him I speak face to face—clearly, not in riddles, / and he beholds the form of the LORD" (Num 12:6–8). The prophet Micah considers Miriam with Moses and Aaron as leaders of the Hebrews out of the land of Egypt (Mic 6:4). The prophetess Miriam died in the wilderness and was buried there (Num 20:1).

**Meditation/Journal**: In your circles of friends, who most resembles the prophetess Miriam? How?

**Canticle Response**: "God is my strength, GOD is my song, / and yes! GOD is my salvation. / *This* is the kind of God I have / and I'm telling the world! / *This* is the God of my father [and mother]— / I'm spreading the news far and wide! / GOD is a fighter, / pure GOD, through and through. / Sing to GOD— / what a victory! / He pitched horse and rider / into the sea." (Exod 15:2–3, 21, TM)

## Moses

**Scripture**: "Never since has there risen a prophet in Israel like Moses, whom the LORD knew face to face. He was unequaled for all the signs and wonders that he LORD sent him to perform in the land of Egypt, against Pharaoh and all his servants and his entire land, and for all the mighty deeds and all the terrifying displays of power that Moses performed in the sight of all Israel." (Deut 34:10–12, NRSVue)

**Reflection**: The HB (OT) book of Deuteronomy (meaning *second law*) is presented as the words of Moses to all Israel before the people cross the Jordan River under the leadership of Moses' successor, Joshua (Deut 1:1). However, after thirty-three chapters, everything changes; the narrator begins to tell about Moses' death (Deut 34:1–8)—quite impossible for Moses himself to do! Then, the narrator adds his own evaluation of Moses, which consists of the above Scripture text. The author of chapter 34 considers Moses to be the greatest prophet in Israel; this means that Moses, as a prophet, spoke to the people for God (Deut 5:27). What made Moses such a great prophet was the fact that the LORD spoke face to face to him (Num 12:8); there was no mediator between God and Moses. No one could equal all the signs and wonders Moses provided in Egypt (Exod 4:1—12:32). Nor could anyone equal the displays of power that Moses performed in the sight of all Israel that are scattered through the HB (OT) books of Exodus, Leviticus, Numbers, and Deuteronomy. However, even in the midst of Moses' greatness, Moses states, "The LORD your God will raise up for you a prophet like me from among your own people; you shall heed such a prophet" (Deut 18:15). Then, the LORD himself speaks: "I will raise up for [the people] a prophet like you from among their own people; I will put my words in the mouth of the prophet, who shall speak to them everything that I command" (Deut 18:18).

**Meditation/Journal**: Whom do you consider to have been the greatest prophet in your family? Who was his or her successor?

**Psalm Response**: "Hallelujah! / Thank GOD! Pray to him by name! / Tell everyone you meet what he has done! / Sing him songs, belt out hymns, translate his wonders into music! / Honor his holy name with Hallelujahs, / you who seek GOD. Live a happy life! / Keep your eyes open for GOD, watch for his words; / be alert for signs of his presence. / . . . [H]e sent his servant Moses, / and Aaron, whom he also chose [, to his people in Egypt]. / They worked marvels in that spiritual wasteland, / miracles in the Land of Ham. / He led Israel out, their arms filled with loot, / and not one among his tribes even stumbled. / Egypt was glad to have them go— / they were scared to death of them." (Ps 105:1–5, 26–27, 37–38, TM)

## Nahum

**Scripture**: "An oracle concerning Nineveh. The book of the vision of Nahum . . . ." (Nah 1:1, NRSVue)

**Reflection**: Nineveh was the capital of Assyria, one of Israel's neighbors. As a superpower of the ancient world, Assyria dominated—or attempted to dominate—the weaker countries around it. The prophet Nahum's vision—a supernatural experience where God communicated with him while he was awake about his judgment on Nineveh for its cruelties to its neighbors—begins the book. Nineveh became the capital of Assyria during the reign of Sennacherib (704–681 BCE); it fell to the Medes and Babylonians in 612 BCE. The reader must keep in mind that the prophet Nahum was a citizen of a country—Israel—that had been cruelly oppressed by Nineveh. The prophet's vengeance comes through his portrayal of God as being jealous, avenging, and wrathful, taking vengeance on his adversaries and raging against his enemies (Nah 1:2). Nahum was most likely written between 663 and 612 BCE, that is, during the reigns of the kings of Judah: Manasseh (687–642 BCE), Amon (642–640 BCE), and Josiah 640–608 BCE), and long after Israel's (Samaria's) fall to Assyria in 722 BCE. Because Nahum's prophecy (vision) about Nineveh falling to its enemies occurred, he is considered a prophet; his book consists of three chapters usually printed in Bibles on the same number of pages. The author of the OT (A) book of Tobit portrays Tobit declaring, ". . . I believe the word of God that Nahum spoke about Nineveh, that all these things will occur and will happen to Assyria and Nineveh" (Tob 14:4, NRSVue). Also, Nahum is mentioned in the Second Book of Esdras (1:40) in the OT (A).

**Meditation/Journal**: Whom would you consider to be like Nahum today? Explain.

**Poem Response**: "GOD's orders on Nineveh: / 'You're the end of the line. / It's all over with Nineveh. / I'm gutting your temple. / Your gods and goddesses go in the trash. / I'm digging your grave. It's an unmarked grave. / You're nothing—no, you're *less* than nothing.' / Look! Striding across the mountains— / a messenger bringing the latest good news: peace! / A holiday, Judah! Celebrate! / Worship and recommit to God! / No more worries about *this* enemy. / This one is history. Close the books." (Nah 1:14–15, TM)

## Nathan

**Scripture**: ". . . [T]he word of the LORD came to Nathan, 'Go and tell my servant David: Thus says the LORD: . . . [T]he LORD declares to you that the LORD will make you a house. . . . I will raise up your offspring after you, . . . and I will establish his kingdom. He shall build a house for my name, and I will establish the throne of his kingdom forever. Your house and your kingdom shall be made sure forever before me; your throne shall be established forever.' . . . [T]his vision Nathan spoke to David." (2 Sam 7:4–5a, 11b–13, 16–17, NRSVue)

**Reflection**: Nathan enters the Second Book of Samuel at the beginning of chapter 7, where the narrator states that David spoke to the prophet Nathan (2 Sam 7:2). Nathan is the earliest example of the court prophet, who served within the royal court of a king as an advisor, messenger of God, and political influencer. Court prophets, like Nathan, were a part of the king's inner circle, offering guidance and interpreting the LORD's will. After David presents his proposal to Nathan to build a temple for the ark of God that was housed in a tent in Jerusalem, Nathan reports to him that God does not want him to build a temple. In the divine plan, God will build a house or royal line for David; one of David's sons will be responsible for building a temple. God promises David that his descendants and kingdom are established forever.

The court prophet has a freedom to speak to the king as does Nathan, when he confronts King David for his adultery with Bathsheba (2 Sam 11:1–5) and death of Uriah (2 Sam 11:6–27) by telling him a story (2 Sam 12:1–6) and letting him know that he knows what David did (2 Sam 12:7–15). As court prophet (1 Kgs 1:8), Nathan appears in the First Book of Kings counseling Bathsheba to go to the dying David and have him proclaim their son Solomon as David's successor (1 Kgs 1:11—2:9). Nathan demonstrates that he is a political insider by creating a plan to convince David that Solomon is the right choice for king of all Israel (1 Kgs 1:11–31).

**Meditation/Journal**: Today, who serves as court prophet in your town, city, county, state, and country? What does he or she do? Explain.

**Prayer Response**: "Who am I, my Master GOD, and what is my family, that you have brought me to this place in life? You know me, Master GOD, just as I am. You've done all this not because of who I am but because of who you are—out of your very heart!—but you've let me in on it. This is what makes you so great, Master GOD! There is none like you, no God but you, nothing to compare with what we've heard with our own ears." (2 Sam 7:18, 20b–22, TM)

## Noadiah

**Scripture**: "Remember . . . , O my God, according to these things that they did, and also Noadiah the prophetess and the rest of the prophets who wanted to make me afraid." (Neh 6:14, NRSVue)

**Reflection**: In all of biblical literature, the prophetess Noadiah makes but one appearance in the HB (OT) book of Nehemiah. Nehemiah, Persian King Artaxerxes' cupbearer (Neh 1:11c), volunteered to go to Jerusalem to help the Jews, who had returned to Jerusalem after Babylonian captivity, rebuild the city walls. With him went Sanballat and Tobiah, officers of the army and calvary, who were displeased that someone had been sent to help the Jews (Neh 2:10). According to Nehemiah's record, his enemies think that because he is rebuilding the wall, the Jews are preparing to rebel and establish Nehemiah as their king (Neh 6:1–6) along with prophets in Jerusalem who would proclaim him king (Neh 6:7). Nehemiah understands that they are attempting to frighten him to stop work on the wall. The next part of the plot is a rumor that Nehemiah's enemies are plotting to kill him, but he concludes that Sanballat and Tobiah have hired the false messenger to intimidate him (Neh 6:10–13).

After having foiled his enemies, Nehemiah utters a short prayer to God—the above Scripture passage—asking him to remember (and punish) Sanballat, Tobiah, the prophetess Noadiah, and all the other prophets who were involved in the plot to make him afraid. Thus, it looks like Noadiah was involved—issuing oracles of intimidation?—in the plot against him.

**Meditation/Journal**: In your lifetime, whom have you discovered to be in a plot against you? Explain.

**Psalm Response**: "My God, don't turn a deaf ear to my hallelujah prayer. / Liars are pouring out invective on me; / Their lying tongues are like a pack of dogs out to get me, / barking their hate, nipping my heels—and for no reason! / I loved them and now they slander me—yes, me!— / and treat my prayer like a crime; / They return my good with evil, / they return my love with hate. / Oh, GOD, my Lord, step in; / work a miracle for me—you can do it!" (Ps 109:1–5, 21, TM)

## Noah

**Scripture**: ". . . Noah found favor in the sight of the LORD. . . . God said to Noah, 'I have determined to make an end of all flesh . . . . Make yourself an ark; . . . make rooms in the ark, and cover it inside and out with pitch. Make a roof for the ark . . . . I am going to bring a flood of waters on the earth, to destroy from under heaven all flesh in which is the breath of life . . . . And of every living thing, of all flesh, you shall bring two of every kind into the ark, to keep them alive with you; they shall be male and female.' Noah did this; he did all that God commanded him. Then the LORD said to Noah, 'Go into the ark, you and all your household, for I have seen that you alone are righteous before me in this generation.'" (Gen 6:8, 13a, 14, 16a, 17, 19, 22; 7:1, NRSVue)

**Reflection**: Noah, even though he is never identified as a prophet in biblical literature, is considered a prophet because he received the LORD's instructions and acted on them. Noah's building of the ark was a prophetic action of warning others about the disastrous flood that was about to take place. The prophet Ezekiel states that he was righteous, meaning that he and God possessed a healthy relationship (Ezek 14:14, 20), and the author of the OT (A) book of Sirach declares that he was perfect and righteous (Sir 44:17–18). In the CB (NT), the author of the Letter to the Hebrews states that he was warned by God about the flood, and he respected the warning and built the ark; thus he was righteous (Heb 11:7). He is mentioned in the CB (NT) First Letter of Peter as building the ark, while God waited patiently for him to do so (1 Pet 3:20), and in the Second Letter of Peter he is declared righteous again (2 Pet

2:5). Some Bibles, like *The Access Bible* (updated edition), feature a chart of the two biblical versions of the flood story (Yahwist and Priestly) that have been melded into one by the author of the HB (OT) book of Genesis from 6:1 through 9:28.

**Meditation/Journal**: Whom do you consider to be righteous, like Noah?

**Psalm Response**: "Get insurance with GOD and do a good deed, / settle down and stick to your last. / Keep company with GOD, / get in on the best. / Less is more and more is less. / One righteous will outclass fifty wicked, / For the wicked are moral weaklings / but the righteous are GOD-strong. / GOD keeps track of the decent folk; / what they do won't soon be forgotten. / Wicked borrows and never returns; / Righteous gives and gives. / Righteous chews on wisdom like a dog on a bone, / rolls virtue around on his tongue. / His heart pumps God's Word like blood through his veins; / his feet are as sure as a cat's." (Ps 37:3–4, 16–18, 21, 30–31, TM)

# 6

# O–S

## FROM OBADIAH TO SIMON MAGUS

### Obadiah

**Scripture**: "The vision of Obadiah. / Thus says the Lord GOD concerning Edom: / We have heard a report from the LORD, / and a messenger has been sent among the nations: / 'Rise up! Let us rise against it for battle!' / I will surely make you least among the nations; / you shall be utterly despised. / Your proud heart has deceived you, / you who live in the clefts of the rock, / whose dwelling is in the heights. / You say in your heart, / 'Who will bring me down to the ground?' / Though you soar aloft like the eagle, / though your nest is set among the stars, / from there I will bring you down, / says the LORD." (Obad 1:1–4)

**Reflection**: The prophet Obadiah's twenty-one verse book occupies two pages in most Bibles between the prophet Amos and the prophet Jonah; because it consists of only one chapter, it is easy to miss. While the prophet begins with a vision—a supernatural auditory experience—from God concerning Edom, a nation descended from Esau—one of the two sons of Isaac; the other being Jacob—the bordering nation, according to Obadiah, has betrayed its Israelite neighbor. In the passage above, Obadiah announces the divine sentence for

Edom's crimes. The divine messenger urges other nations to rise up against Edom and destroy it. He declares that the Edomites have been deceived by their pride and their location—in the mountains to the east of the Jordan Valley. The Edomites are characterized by their lofty dwellings in the mountains, but Obadiah presents the LORD declaring that he will bring them down to the ground. Biblical scholars think the short book was written after the Babylonians destroyed Jerusalem in 586/587 BCE, because after that the Edomites took advantage of Judah's weakness by betraying the survivors (Obad 1:11, 14). The book ends with the reverse of what the Edomites did in Judah; the Jewish returnees are prophesied to bring about Edom's end (Obad 1:15–21).

**Meditation/Journal**: In your life, who in your family has betrayed you? Explain.

**Prophetic Response**: "'Oh, [thieves will] take Esau apart, piece by piece, / empty his purse and pockets. / All your old partners will drive you to the edge. / Your old friends will lie to your face. / Your old drinking buddies will stab you in the back. / Your world will collapse. You won't know what hit you. / So don't be surprised'—it's GOD's sure Word!— / 'Because of the murderous history compiled / against your brother Jacob. / You will be looked down on by everyone. / You'll lose your place in history. / On that day you stood there and didn't do anything. / Strangers took your brother's army into exile. / Godless foreigners invaded and pillaged Jerusalem. / You stood there and watched. / You were as bad as they were.'" (Obad 1:6–8, 10–11, TM)

## Oded

**Scripture**: "The people of Israel took captive two hundred thousand of their kin: women, sons, and daughters; they also took much spoil from them and brought the spoil to Samaria. But a prophet of the LORD was there whose name was Oded; he went out to meet the army that came to Samaria and said to them, 'Because the LORD, the God of your ancestors, was angry with Judah, he gave them into your hand, but you have killed them in a rage that has reached up to heaven. Now hear me, and send back the captives whom you have taken from your kindred, for the fierce wrath of the LORD is upon you.'" (2 Chr 28:8–9, 11, NRSVue)

**Reflection**: During the reign of King Ahaz of Judah (732–716 BCE), he was defeated in battle by the king of Aram (2 Chr 28:5) and the King of Israel, Pekah (740–732 BCE) (2 Chr 28:6). The chronicler attributes the defeat of Judah because the king and people had abandoned the LORD, the God of their ancestors (2 Chr 28:6). As noted in the Scripture text above, Israel took 200,000

Judeans in the south, kinfolk of Israel in the north, along with lots of spoil to the capital of the Northern Kingdom of Israel: Samaria. While the Judeans were on the march to Samaria, the prophet Oded went, on his own initiative, to meet the army escorting the captives of war. He explained that the army had captives because God was angry with Judah. He realized that they were going to make the Judeans slaves of Israel (2 Chr 28:10). So, on his own initiative he told the army to send back their kinfolk captives; otherwise, the LORD's wrath would be upon them. Almost immediately, the army abandoned the captives and the spoil, and the assembly's officials clothed the naked captives, gave them sandals, provided food and drink, and anointed them. Then, they led them to Jericho, the frontier, from which they could reenter Judah (2 Chr 28:15). Oded, without any royal backing saw to getting the Judean captives and spoil back to Judah by confronting the army of Israel.

**Meditation/Journal**: In your life, whom do you know who took the initiative to take care of the homeless, the naked, the hungry, the thirsty, etc.?

**Psalm Response**: "All my life long I'll praise GOD, / singing songs to my God as long as I live. / Don't put your life in the hands of experts / who know nothing of life, of *salvation* life. / Instead, get help from . . . God . . . , / put your hope in GOD and know real blessing! / He always does what he says— / he defends the wronged, / he feeds the hungry. / GOD frees prisoners— / he gives sight to the blind, / he lifts up the fallen. / God loves good people, protects strangers, / takes the side of orphans and widows, / but makes short work of the wicked." (Ps 146:2–3, 5, 7–9, TM)

## Old Prophet

**Scripture**: ". . . [T]here lived an old prophet in Bethel. . . . [H]e said to his sons, 'Saddle a donkey for me.' So they saddled a donkey for him, and he mounted it. He went after the man of God [who had come from Judah to Bethel] and found him sitting under an oak tree. Then he said to him, 'Come home with me and eat some food.' But he said, 'I cannot return with you or go in with you, nor will I eat food or drink water with you in this place, for it was said to me by the word of the LORD, "You shall not eat food or drink water there . . . ."' Then the other said to him, 'I also am a prophet as you are, and an angel spoke to me by the word of the LORD, "Bring him back with you into your house so that he may eat food and drink water."' But he was deceiving him."(1 Kgs 13:11a, 13–14a, 15–18, NRSVue)

**Reflection**: It is very difficult to remember two unnamed characters in the same biblical story who are identified only as a man of God and an old prophet! Earlier in chapter 13 of the First Book of Kings, a man of God was sent to Bethel to confront King Jeroboam I of Israel (931–910 BCE), who was worshiping one of the gold calves he had erected in Bethel (2 Kgs 12:25–33). After confronting Jeroboam, the man of God headed home, stopping only to rest under an oak tree, which is where the old prophet found him. The man of God knew that he was not supposed to take food nor drink from the king (2 Kgs 13:9), nor from anyone else (1 Kgs 13:16). However, after the old prophet identified himself as a fellow prophet to the man of God and informed him that he had received a divine revelation, the man of God went with him to his house, where he ate food and drank water. During the meal, the word of God came to the old prophet: "Thus says the LORD: Because you have disobeyed the word of the LORD and have not kept the commandment that the LORD your God commanded you but have come back and have eaten food and drunk water in the place of which he said to you, 'Eat no food, and drink no water,' your body shall not come to your ancestral tomb" (2 Kgs 13:20–22). After the man of God left the old prophet's house, he was met by a lion on the road who killed him (2 Kgs 13:24). Thus, the old prophet's words came true. The old prophet found his body, brought it back to where he lived, and buried it in his own grave (2 Kgs 13:29–30). While the man of God should have obeyed the LORD rather than trusting the old prophet, the man of God's prophecy about the altar in Bethel being torn down by King Josiah (640–608 BCE) (1 Kgs 13:1–3) was fulfilled (2 Kgs 23:15–18). While the biblical author gives no motive for the old prophet's lie to the man of God, both of their prophecies are fulfilled.

**Meditation/Journal**: What bothers you about the story of the man of God and the old prophet? Explain.

**Psalm Response**: "Quick, GOD, I need your helping hand! / The last decent person just went down, / All the friends I depended on gone. / Everyone talks in lie language; / Lies slide off their oily lips. / They doubletalk with forked tongues. / God's words are pure words, / Pure silver words refined seven times / In the fires of his word-kiln, / Pure on earth as well as in heaven." (Ps 12:1–2, 6, TM)

## Paul

**Scripture**: ". . . I [, Paul,] want you to know, brothers and sisters, that the gospel that was proclaimed to me is not of human origin, for I did not receive it from a human source, nor was I taught it, but I received it through a revelation of Jesus Christ." (Gal 1:11–12, NRSVue)

**Reflection**: In his CB (NT) letter to the Galatians, Paul explains that the gospel he preached was not good news delivered by the preaching or teaching of another human being. It was revealed to him, like messages were revealed to prophets, by Jesus Anointed. While Paul is primarily known as an apostle in the CB (NT), his writings often contain prophetic themes and language, as noted above. Furthermore, his own narration of his call echoes that of prophetic calls elsewhere in biblical literature: ". . . [W]hen the one who had set me apart before I was born and called me through his grace was pleased to reveal his Son to me, so that I might proclaim him among the gentiles, I did not confer with any human . . ." (Gal 1:15–16, NRSVue). Besides Paul's narration of his call to be a prophet to the gentiles, the author of the Acts of the Apostles narrates his call three different times (Acts 9:1–22; 22:6–16; 26:12–18). Like prophets in the HB (OT) were given a mission and what to say from God, Paul was given a mission to proclaim Jesus Anointed to gentiles. Thus, Paul, who received a direct revelation, like the prophets in the HB (OT) did, shared the message he received from God (Jesus) with others about his understanding of God's advanced plan of salvation for both Jews and gentiles. Also, Paul imitated the prophets Elijah and Elisha, when Eutychus fell into a deep sleep and fell out a window to the ground three floors below, and he was presumed dead, until Paul took him into his arms and announced that life was still in him (Acts 20:9–12).

**Meditation/Journal**: What do you understand as Paul's preaching of God's advanced plan of salvation for both Jews and gentiles?

**Psalm Response**: "God's glory is on tour in the skies . . . . / . . . [W]ords aren't heard, / . . . voices aren't recorded. / But . . . silence fills the earth; / unspoken truth is spoken everywhere. / That's how God's Word vaults across the skies / from sunrise to sunset, / Melting ice, scorching deserts, / warming hearts to faith. / The revelation of GOD is whole / and pulls our lives together. (Ps 19:1a, 3–4, 6–7, TM)

## Peter

**Scripture**: ". . . Fellow Jews and all who live in Jerusalem, let this be known to you, and listen to what I say. Indeed, these [men] are not drunk, as you suppose, for it is only nine o'clock in the morning. No, this is what was spoken through the prophet Joel: / In the last days it will be, God declares, / that I will pour out my Spirit upon all flesh . . . ." (Acts 2:14–17ab)

**Reflection**: While Peter is usually understood to be an apostle, in the CB (NT) Acts of the Apostles he is presented as a prophet who interprets other prophets. After the author narrates the events of Pentecost (Acts 2:1–12), he brings Peter into the scene to answer the question, "What does this mean?" (Acts 2:12, NRSVue), while others, who hear apostles speaking in foreign languages, conclude that they are filled with new wine or drunk (Acts 2:13). Peter dismisses the accusation that they are drunk by noting that it was only nine o'clock in the morning! Then he proceeds to show how the prophet Joel's words are filled with God's gift of the Spirit, which has been poured out on all flesh. In other words, the different languages being spoken and heard prove Joel's prophecy; Peter is a prophet because he names the prophecy as being fulfilled. The divinely inspired message of Joel has become Peter's divinely inspired message, and Peter has become the divinely inspired messenger. And such is the character of Peter in the Acts of the Apostles.

However, there is another Peter character found in the two Letters of Peter. Biblical scholars do not think that the historical Peter wrote those letters; someone wrote them in Peter's name so that they would carry the authority of the historical Peter. In the Second Letter of Peter, the author exhorts his readers to remember "the words spoken in the past by the holy prophets" (2 Pet 3:2) concerning two events which had not yet happened. The first concerned the day of the Lord coming like a thief (2 Pet 3:1–10). The second concerned the destruction of the heavens and the earth with fire (2 Pet 3:7, 11–13). The author concluded his letter by telling his readers to wait, as they had been forewarned by him (2 Pet 3:14–18). In other words, the message of the Peter character in the two Letters of Peter has not yet been fulfilled. Not to be forgotten are the different Peter characters appearing in the four gospels.

**Meditation/Journal**: Of all the Peter characters in the CB (NT)—Mark, Matthew, Luke, John, Acts, 1 & 2 Peter—which is your favorite? Why?

**Psalm Response**: "I look to you, heaven-dwelling God, / look up to you for help. / Like servants, alert to their master's commands, / like a maiden attending her lady, / We're watching and waiting, holding our breath, / awaiting your word of mercy. / Mercy, GOD, mercy! (Ps 123:1–3a, TM)

## Philip

**Scripture**: ". . . [A]n angel of the Lord said to Philip, 'Get up and go toward the south to the road that goes down from Jerusalem to Gaza.' . . . So he got up and went. Now there was an Ethiopian eunuch, a court official of the Candace, the queen of the Ethiopians, in charge of her entire treasury . . . seated in his chariot; he was reading the prophet Isaiah. Then the Spirit said to Philip, 'Go over to this chariot and join it.' So Philip ran up to it and heard him reading the prophet Isaiah. He asked, 'Do you understand what you are reading?' He replied, 'How can I, unless someone guides me?' And he invited Philip to get in and sit beside him. Now the passage of the scripture that he was reading was this: 'Like a sheep he was led to the slaughter, / and like a lamb silent before its shearer, / so he does not open his mouth.' The eunuch asked Philip, 'About whom may I ask you, does the prophet say this, about himself or about someone else?' Then Philip began to speak, and starting with this scripture he proclaimed to him the good news about Jesus. . . . [T]he Spirit of the Lord snatched Philip away . . . ." (Acts 8:26–32, 34–35, 39, NRSVue)

**Reflection**: While Philip is better known as an apostle in the CB (NT), in the Acts of the Apostles he is portrayed as a prophet. Like HB (OT) prophets, he is sent by God, who, in the text, is described as an angel of the Lord. Furthermore, the Spirit speaks to him (Acts 8:29), and the Spirit snatches him away (Acts 8:39). Philip is a messenger of God sent to the Ethiopian eunuch, who is reading aloud from the prophet Isaiah. Philip fulfills his role as an apostle—one sent—to teach God's word by interpreting Isaiah 53:7 as referring to Jesus' death. Then, after coming upon some water, he baptizes the eunuch into the death of Jesus. Thus, Philip's actions indicate that he is a prophet, a divinely-sent messenger, who communicates God's will to the eunuch and brings about his spiritual transformation through baptism in the CB (NT) Acts of the Apostles.

While not being referred to as a prophet in the CB (NT) gospel according to John, Philip also functions as a prophet by bringing Nathanael to Jesus; he fulfills the prophetic task of pointing others towards God. After the Johannine Jesus calls Philip to follow him (John 1:43), Philip found Nathanael and said to him, "We have found him about whom Moses in the Law and also the Prophets wrote, Jesus son of Joseph from Nazareth" (John 1:45 , NRSVue). Then, Philip invited Nathanael to go with him and see Jesus. Not only is Philip fulfilling his prophetic role as a messenger of God, but he is illustrating a characteristic or motif of the fourth gospel; once someone is called by Jesus, that person goes and calls another person. In other words, Philip points Nathanael towards the divine, thus demonstrating a prophetic spirit of sharing good news and leading others to a relationship with God through Jesus.

**Meditation/Journal**: What do you think is Philip's strongest aspect as a prophet? How is that aspect present in your life?

**Psalm Response**: "The God of gods—it's GOD!—speaks out, shouts, 'Earth!' / welcomes the sun in the east, / farewells the disappearing sun in the west. / . . . God blazes into view. / Our God makes his entrance, / he's not shy in his coming. / Starbursts of fireworks precede him. / He summons heaven and earth as a jury . . . . / 'Are you listening, dear people? I'm getting ready to speak . . . . / This is God, your God, / speaking to you. / Spread for me a banquet of praise, / serve High God a feast of kept promises, / And call for help when you're in trouble— / I'll help you, and you'll honor me.'" (Ps 50:1–4a, 7, 14–15, TM)

## Quake

Scripture: "The words of Amos, who was among the shepherds of Tekoa, which he saw concerning Israel in the days of King Uzziah of Judah and in the days of King Jeroboam son of Joash of Israel, two years before the earthquake." (Amos 1:1, NRSVue)

**Reflection**: The verb *to quake* means *to shake, to tremble,* or *to rock*. It is often paired with earth—earthquake—to indicate a shaking, trembling, or rocking of the tectonic plates of the earth, called a tremor. In biblical texts, earthquakes are frequently associated with prophetic warnings and divine manifestations. For example, the narrator of the HB (OT) book of Exodus notes that after the LORD descended upon Mount Sinai (Horeb), "the whole mountain shook violently" (Exod 19:18, NRSVue). The prophet Amos dates his prophetic utterances two years before a great earthquake, during the reigns of King Uzziah (Azariah) of Judah (767–740 BCE) and King Jeroboam II of Israel (782–753 BCE). Indeed, according to archeologists and archaeological evidence, there was a major earthquake in the mid-eighth century BCE. The prophet Zechariah also mentions the earthquake (Zech 14:5). Prophets, like Amos and Zechariah, use an earthquake, which in the ancient world could not be predicted or controlled, as a sign of God's power. In the CB (NT), the author of Matthew's Gospel states that after Jesus died "the earth shook" (Matt 27:51b, NRSVue) and says there was "a great earthquake" (Matt 28:3, NRSVue) to herald the resurrection. The prophet Nahum used the earthquake in a similar fashion to herald the LORD's coming, writing, "The mountains quake before him . . . , / the earth heaves before him . . ." (Nah 1:5, NRSVue), just like the prophet Isaiah states that when the LORD came down from heaven, "the mountains quaked at [his] presence" (Isa 64:3, NRSVue).

**Meditation/Journal**: When you hear about an earthquake, what do you conclude?

**Psalm Response**: "After Israel left Egypt, / The mountains turned playful and skipped like rams, / the hills frolicked like spring lambs. / What's wrong with you . . . mountains, why did you skip like rams? / and you, hills, frolic like spring lambs? / Tremble, Earth! You're in the Lord's presence! / in the presence of . . . God." (Ps 114:1a, 4–7, TM)

## Ramah

**Scripture**: "Thus says the LORD: / A voice is heard in Ramah, / lamentation and bitter weeping. / Rachel is weeping for her children; / she refuses to be comforted for her children, / because they are no more. / Thus says the LORD: / Keep your voice from weeping / and your eyes from tears, / for there is a reward for your work, / says the LORD: / they shall come back from the land of the enemy; / there is hope for your future, / says the LORD: / your children shall come back to their own country." (Jer 31:15–17, NRSVue)

**Reflection**: Ramah is not the name of a prophet; it is the name of a hilltop village near Jerusalem in the ancient territory of Benjamin (Josh 18:25; Neh 11:33). Rachel, wife of Jacob, is the mother of Benjamin and Joseph; in the prophet Jeremiah, she is weeping for her children—the residents of the Benjaminite territory—because Nebuchadnezzar, King of Babylon, had captured the Kingdom of Judah, composed of the two tribes of Judah and Benjamin, and taken every able-bodied man, woman, and child as captives of war to be resettled in Babylon. However, according to Jeremiah's prophecy, the LORD tells the mourners to stop weeping for the children (citizens), because one day they will return to the kingdom of Judah. The last two verses of the above Scripture text (Jer 31:16–17) are ignored by the author of Matthew's Gospel, even though they were fulfilled by Cyrus, King of Persia, who, after conquering Babylon, released the Jewish captives and permitted them to return to Judah (2 Chr 36:22–23; Ezra 1:1–5). Unique to Matthew's Gospel is the narrative about King Herod killing "all the children in and around Bethlehem who were two years old or under" (Matt 2:16, NRSVue), and the author's interpretation that his act fulfilled the words of the prophet Jeremiah: "A voice was heard in Ramah, / wailing and loud lamentation, / Rachel weeping for her children; / she refused to be consoled, because they are no more" (Matt 2:18). The Matthean story has nothing to do with Ramah, since the birth of Jesus took place in Bethlehem (Matt 2:5–6, 16). The author of Matthew's Gospel loves fulfillment quotations—HB (OT) verses that are fulfilled, according to him, in his work. However, he is not often accurate, even creating a prophetic utterance in order to fulfill it (Matt2:23)!

**Meditation/Journal**: What person (prophet) in your life lacked accurate proof when telling you something (citing sources) that needed documentation or authentication?

**Psalm Response**: "It seemed like a dream, too good to be true, / when GOD returned [the] exiles. / We laughed, we sang, / we couldn't believe our good fortune. / We were the talk of the nations— / 'GOD was wonderful to them!' /

GOD was wonderful to us; / we are one happy people. / And now GOD, do it again — / So those who went off with heavy hearts / will come home laughing, with armloads of blessing." (Ps 125:1–3, 4a, 6, TM)

## Samuel

**Scripture**: "As Samuel grew up, the LORD was with him and let none of his words fall to the ground. And all Israel . . . knew that Samuel was a trustworthy prophet of the LORD. The LORD continued to appear at Shiloh, for the LORD revealed himself to Samuel at Shiloh by the word of the LORD. And the word of Samuel came to all Israel." (1 Sam 3:19—4:1a, NRSVue)

**Reflection**: The prophet who ranks in importance after Moses is Samuel, whose name means *heard* or *asked of God*, referring to his mother Hannah's request for a son from the LORD (1 Sam 1:11a). Not only is Samuel known as a prophet (1 Sam 3:20)—as indicated above—but he was a Nazirite (1 Sam 1:11); he did not drink wine or intoxicants, and no razor touched his head (1 Sam 1:11b). Also, Samuel was the last of the judges (1 Sam 7:3–6), a priest at Shiloh, where the ark was kept until King David moved it to Jerusalem (1 Sam 1:27–28; 9:13), a seer (1 Sam 9:9), and the anointer of the first king of Israel—Saul—(1 Sam 10:1) and the second king of Israel—David—(1 Sam 16:13). The two books of Samuel are focused on the beginning of the monarchy and named after Samuel because of the huge role he played in establishing it. It was most likely written after 586/587 BCE during the Babylonian exile, when an effort was made to collect Israel's history and traditions, in which the prophet Samuel plays an important part. Thus, the two books of Samuel are filled with prophetic utterances and enacted prophecies. Even after he dies (1 Sam 25:1; 28:3a), Samuel has a prophetic role to play (1 Sam 28:3b–25); he reminds Saul that the LORD has taken away his throne and given it to David (2 Sam 5:1–5).

**Meditation/Journal**: Whom have you known to wear many hats, like Samuel?

**Psalm Response**: "All we are and have we owe to GOD, / Holy God of Israel, our King! / A long time ago you spoke in a vision, / you spoke to your faithful beloved: / 'I've crowned a hero, / I chose the best I could find. / I found David, my servant, / poured holy oil on his head, / And I'll keep my hand steadily on him, / yes, I'll stick with him through thick and thin. / I am with him for good and I'll love him forever; / I've set him on high—he's riding high! / Yes, I'm setting him apart as the First of the royal line, / High King over all of earth's kings. / I'll preserve him eternally in my love, / I'll faithfully do all I so solemnly promised.'" (Ps 89:18–21, 24, 27–29, TM)

## Seventy Elders of Israel

**Scripture**: ". . . Moses . . . told the people [of Israel] the words of the LORD, and he gathered seventy of the elders of the people and placed them all around the tent [of meeting]. Then the LORD came down in the cloud and spoke to him and took some of the spirit that was on him and put it on the seventy elders, and when the spirit rested upon them, they prophesied." (Num 11:24–25a, NRSVue)

**Reflection**: After the work of governing the people of Israel took a toll on Moses and he pleaded for the LORD to help him, the LORD instructed him to gather seventy elders and officers of Israel and bring them to the tent of meeting (Num 11:10–23). Once the unnamed seventy men take their place around the tent of meeting, the LORD appears in the form of a cloud (Num 9:15), speaking to Moses, and taking some of the spirit that was on Moses and putting it on the seventy; once the divine spirit rested upon the seventy, they became prophets, like Moses, and temporarily mediated messages from the LORD. Their period of prophesying does not last, however, because the author of the HB (OT) book of Numbers wants to imply that Moses remains the only authoritative prophet or meditator of the LORD's words. Nothing else is said about the group of seventy, nor are any words of their prophesy recorded. In the CB (NT), the author of Luke's Gospel employs this account to depict Jesus uniquely appointing seventy in pairs to visit places and towns he intended to go (Luke 10:1–24). In other words, the author of Luke's Gospel presents his Jesus character as a new Moses, depicting him doing what the LORD did through Moses.

**Meditation/Journal**: Whom do you identify as the elders endowed with the spirit in your life?

**Psalm Response**: "GOD, my God, how great you are! / beautifully, gloriously robed . . . . / What a wildly wonderful world, GOD! / You made it all, with Wisdom at your side, / made earth overflow with your wonderful creations. / All the creatures look expectantly to you / to give them their meals on time. / If you turned your back, / they'd die in a minute— / revert to original mud; / Send out your Spirit and they spring to life— / the whole countryside in bloom and blossom. / The glory of GOD—let it last forever! / Let GOD enjoy his creation!" (Ps 104:1a, 24, 27, 29–31, TM)

## Shemaiah 1

**Scripture**: ". . . [T]he word of God came to Shemaiah the man of God. 'Say to King Rehoboam of Judah, son of Solomon, and to all the house of Judah and Benjamin, and to the rest of the people: Thus says the LORD: You shall not go up or fight against your kindred the people of Israel. Let everyone go home, for this thing is from me.' So they heeded the word of the LORD and went home . . . , according to the word of the Lord." (1 Kgs 12:22–24, NRSVue)

**Reflection**: After King Rehoboam became king of Judah (931–913 BCE) after his father Solomon, Jeroboam I established himself as King of Israel (931–910). Rehoboam intended to rally his troops in Jerusalem and go north to fight against Israel, "to restore the kingdom to Rehoboam son of Solomon" (1 Kgs 12:21, NRSVue). However, the prophet Shemaiah appears with the word of the LORD, telling Rehoboam not to do what he intends, because the division of the kingdom into the North (Israel) and South (Judah) is God's doing. If Rehoboam went to fight against Israel, he would be fighting against God. Thus, the plan is abandoned.

A different story featuring the prophet Shemaiah appears in the Second Book of Chronicles. King Shishak of Egypt got ready to attack Jerusalem during Rehoboam's fifth year as king. The prophet Shemaiah told the king: "Thus says the LORD: You abandoned me, so I have abandoned you to the hand of Shishak" (2 Chr 12:5, NRSVue). Shemaiah's words cause the king and his officers to recognize the LORD's truth, and they humble themselves. The word of the LORD came to Shemaiah, "They have humbled themselves; I will not destroy them, but I will grant them some deliverance . . . . Nevertheless, they shall be his servants, so that they may know the difference between serving me and serving the kingdoms of other lands" (2 Kgs 12:7–8, NRSVue). King Shishak took away treasures and shields of gold (2 Chr 12:9). But Rehoboam was spared, as indicated by the prophet Shemaiah.

**Meditation/Journal**: Who has spoken truth to you, like Shemaiah spoke it to King Rehoboam? What change did that facilitate in you?

**Psalm Response**: GOD, "Your righteousness is eternally right, / your revelation is the only truth. / As those out to get me come closer and closer, / they go farther and farther from the truth you reveal; / But you're the closest of all to me, GOD, / and all your judgments true. / Your words all add up to the sum total: Truth. / Your righteous decisions are eternal." (Ps 119:145, 150–151, 160, TM)

## Shemaiah 2

**Scripture**: "To Shemaiah . . . you shall say: Thus says the LORD of hosts, the God of Israel: In your own name you sent letters to all the people who are in Jerusalem . . . , saying, . . . [W]hy have you not rebuked Jeremiah . . . , who plays the prophet for you? For he has actually sent to us in Babylon, saying, 'It will be a long time; build houses and live in them, and plant gardens and eat what they produce.' Then the word of the LORD came to Jeremiah: Send to all the exiles, saying, Thus says the LORD concerning Shemaiah . . . : Because Shemaiah has prophesied to you, though I did not send him, and has led you to trust in a life, therefore thus says the Lord: I am going to punish Shemaiah . . . and his descendants; he shall not have anyone living among this people to see the good that I am going to do to my people, says the LORD, for he has spoken rebellion against the LORD." (Jer 29:24–25, 27–28, 30–32, NRSVue)

**Reflection**: Since there are twenty-four men with the name Shemaiah in biblical literature, it should come as no surprise that there are two prophets bearing the same name. The Shemaiah found in the prophet Jeremiah is one of the exiles in Babylon. He has written to the high priest in Jerusalem, telling him that he should silence the prophet Jeremiah, because he has written to the exiles, telling them that they are going to be in Babylon for a long time (Jer 29:10); so, they should build homes for themselves and live in them, and they should plant gardens and eat the produce from them. The exiles think that the LORD has raised up prophets for them in Babylon (Jer 29:15), among whom is Shemaiah, who doesn't think that the exile will last very long. After hearing Shemaiah's letter, Jeremiah writes his own letter, explaining to the exiles that Shemaiah is lying to them and tricking them into trusting his lie (Jer 29:31). Jeremiah informs the exiles that he did not send Shemaiah to them. Furthermore, the LORD will punish Shemaiah and his descendants; there will be no living descendants to witness what the LORD will do for his people in the future (Jer 29:32). Thus, the prophet Jeremiah labels Shemaiah a false prophet. Shemaiah gave the exiles false hope for a quick release from Babylonian captivity and return to Jerusalem. Jeremiah removes that hope and calls it rebellion against the LORD.

**Meditation/Journal**: Have you ever rebelled against another person or God with a letter, an e-mail, or a text? Explain.

**Psalm Response**: "Listen, dear friends, to God's truth, / bend your ears to what I tell you. / Never forget the works of God / but keep his commands to the letter. / Heaven forbid [children] should be like their parents, / bullheaded and bad, / A fickle and faithless bunch / who never stayed true to God. / But they kept on giving him a hard time, / rebelled against God, the High God, / refused to do anything he told them. / They were worse, if that's possible, than their parents: / traitors—crooked as a corkscrew." (Ps 78:1, 7–8, 56–57, TM)

## Silas

**Scripture**: ". . . Silas, who [was himself a] prophet, said much to encourage and strengthen the brothers and sisters [in Antioch]. After [he] had been there for some time, [he was] sent off in peace by the brothers and sisters to those who had sent [him]." (Acts 15:32–33, NRSVue)

**Reflection**: In the CB (NT) Acts of the Apostles, a council is held in Jerusalem to determine what parts of Jewish Torah the gentiles needed to follow; the major issue was circumcision, a practice not done by gentiles, but a definite practice of Judaism. After discussion, decisions were reached, and a letter was written about the decisions to be sent to Antioch. Silas is one of two men entrusted with the letter. After traveling to Antioch with Paul and Barnabas and with his co-letter carrier—Judas Barsabbas, who, like Silas, is named a prophet (Acts 15:32)—he read the letter to gentile believers in Antioch and spent time encouraging and strengthening them in the faith before traveling back to Jerusalem. At some time after that, Silas joined Paul on a missionary trip (Acts 15:40). Along with Paul, Silas was beaten and put in prison, after Paul exorcised a female slave (Acts 16:16–24), but an earthquake shook open the prison doors, and Paul and Silas went with the jailer to his home, where they converted him and his household. Then, Silas accompanied Paul to Thessalonica (Acts 17:1–9), Beroea (Acts 17:10–15), and Corinth (Acts 18:5–11). While the Greek form of the name is Silas, the Latin form of the name is Silvanus, and he is found mentioned in Paul's Second Letter to the Corinthians (1:19), in Paul's First Letter to the Thessalonians (1:1), in the Second Letter to the Thessalonians (1:1), and the First Letter of Peter (5:12). His name means *lover of words*, which indicates that he not only carried letters from others and read them to the addressees, but may have also written letters, as indicted by 1 Peter 5:12.

**Meditation/Journal**: What is your preferred form of written communication—letter writing, card writing, e-mailing, texting, etc.? What does your preferred form of written communication enable you to do?

**Psalm Response**: "Blessed are you who give yourselves over to GOD, / turn your backs on the world's 'sure thing,' / ignore what the world worships; / The world's a huge stockpile / of GOD-wonders and God-thoughts. / Nothing and no one / comes close to you! / I start talking about you, telling what I know, /

and quickly run out of words. / Neither numbers nor words / account for you. / You've opened my ears / so I can listen. / So I answered, 'I'm coming. / I read in your letter what you wrote about me, / And I'm coming to the party / Your throwing for me' / That's when God's Word entered my life, / became part of my very being." (Ps 40:4–5, 6b–8, TM)

## Simeon Niger

**Scripture**: ". . . [I]n the church at Antioch there were prophets and teachers: . . . Simeon who was called Niger . . . . While they were worshipping the Lord and fasting, the Holy Spirit said, 'Set apart for me Barnabas and Saul for the work to which I have called them.' Then after fasting and praying they laid their hands on them and sent them off." (Acts 13:1–3, NRSVue)

**Reflection**: Simeon, whose name means *hearing with obedience*, is also called Niger, which means *black* or *darky*. This indicates that Simeon either had a dark complexion, or he was of African descent. His names are mentioned only in the CB (NT) Acts of the Apostles, in which he is one of several prophets in Antioch. While worshiping and fasting, they receive a revelation from the Holy Spirit that instructs them to set apart Barnabas and Saul (Paul) by delegating them by laying their hands on their heads. The prophet Simeon Niger, mentioned in the Acts of the Apostles, remains unknown.

**Meditation/Journal**: Who has served you as a prophet and remains unknown to others? What prophetic service did he or she offer you?

**Psalm Response**: "Hallelujah! / You who serve GOD, praise GOD! / Just to speak his name is praise! / Just to remember GOD is a blessing— / now and tomorrow and always. / From east to west, from dawn to dusk, / keep lifting all your praises to GOD. / GOD is higher than anything and anyone, / outshining everything you can see in the skies." (Ps 113:1–4, TM)

## Simeon (of Jerusalem)

**Scripture**: ". . . [T]here was a man in Jerusalem whose name was Simeon; this man was righteous and devout, looking forward to the consolation of Israel, and the Holy Spiri rested on him. It had been revealed to him by the Holy Spirit that he would not see death before he had seen the Lord's Messiah. Guided by the Spirit, Simeon came into the temple, and when the parents brought in the child Jesus . . . , Simeon took him in his arms and praised God . . . ." (Luke 2:25–28, NRSVue)

**Reflection**: Simeon of Jerusalem is a unique prophetic character in Luke's Gospel in the CB (NT) who made but one appearance. Like prophets in the HB (OT), Simeon received a revelation that he would not die until he saw the Lord's Messiah, the Lord's Anointed. As the author of Luke's Gospel unfolded the story, Simeon recognized the child Jesus as the Anointed One. Like many other characters in Luke's Gospel, Simeon uttered a prophecy that served as a programmatic text: "This child is destined for the falling and the rising of many in Israel, and to be a sign that will be opposed so that the inner thoughts of many will be revealed . . . (Luke 2:34–35, NRSVue). That prophecy was fulfilled in the remainder of the twenty-four-chapter book. Finally, Simeon prophesized that the child's mother's—Mary—soul—best understood as her inner spirit—would be pierced with a sword (Luke 2:38), a reference to Jesus' crucifixion and death (Luke 23:26–49, 55). Simeon's first prophecy about not dying until he had seen the Messiah was fulfilled, as he recognizes the child Jesus to be a light of revelation to the gentiles and the glory of the Israelites (Luke 2:32). In order to find the fulfillment of Simeon's second and third prophecies, one must read the rest of Luke's Gospel. Just as quickly as the Spirit-filled Simeon appeared in the narrative, he, likewise, disappeared; he fulfilled his Lucan role of being a prophet and setting forth the outline for the rest of the gospel.

**Meditation/Journal**: In your lifetime, who has appeared for a short time, spoken important words to you, and then disappeared?

**Canticle Response**: "God, you can now release your servant; / release me in peace as you promised. / With my own eyes I've seen your salvation; / it's now out in the open for everyone to see: / A God-revealing light to the non-Jewish nations, / and of glory for your people Israel." (Luke 2:29–32, TM)

## Simon Magus

**Scripture**: ". . .[A] certain man named Simon had previously practiced magic in the city and amazed the people of Samaria, saying that he was someone great. All of them from the least to the greatest, listened to him eagerly saying, 'This man is the power of God that is called Great.' And they listened eagerly to him because for a long time he had amazed them with his magic. Even Simon himself believed. After being baptized, he . . . was amazed when he saw the signs and great miracles that took place. Now when Simon saw that the Spirit was given through the laying on of the apostles' hands, he offered them money, saying, 'Give me also this power so that anyone on whom I lay my hands may receive the Holy Spirit.' But Peter said to him, 'May your silver perish with you, because you thought you could obtain God's gift with money! You have no part or share in this, for your heart is not right before God.' Simon answered, 'Pray for me to the Lord, that nothing of what you have said may happen to me.'" (Acts 8:9–11, 13, 18–21, 24)

**Reflection**: Simon Magus (Magician) is a prophet-want-a-be! As the narrator of the story makes clear, Simon did not call himself great; the people of Samaria reached the conclusion that he possessed the power of God after observing his magic. The narrator does not even name him a false prophet. In the course of the story, the great magician Simon, who had won over many Samaritans, was quickly reduced to a mere convert! After observing that the Spirit was given through the laying on of hands, Simon, who remained at heart a magician, desired to buy that power to enhance his magical capabilities and either live up to the Samaritans' estimation of him as great or to enhance further his greatness! Peter serves the author's goal of making clear that Christianity has nothing in common with magic. Furthermore, miracles, magic, and money are elements of power; however, only God can wield power (Spirit) properly. That is why Peter curses the want-a-be-prophet, and Simon the magician—who is now less great than he was before!—requests prayers that nothing else will happen to him. Peter tells Simon to pray "to the Lord that, if possible, the intent of [his] heart may be forgiven [him]" (Acts 8:22, NRSVue), if he repents (Acts 8:22).

**Meditation/Journal**: Whom have you known was a want-a-be-prophet wanting to wield divine power like Simon Magus? Explain.

**Psalm Response**: "All together now—applause for God! / Sing songs to the tune of his glory, / set glory to the rhythms of his praise. / Say of God, 'We've never seen anything like him!' / When your enemies see you in action, / they slink off like scolded dogs. / The whole earth falls to its knees— / it worships you, sings to you, / can't stop enjoying your name and fame." (Ps 66:1–4, TM)

**B**iblical **P**rophets

# **T** to **Z**

# 7

# T–Z

## FROM TEACHERS TO ZEPHANIAH

### Teachers

**Scripture**: "When [Tobit] was about to die, he called his son Tobias and . . . gave this command: . . . '[E]verything that was spoken by the prophets of Israel whom God sent will occur. None of all their words will fail, but all will come true at their appointed times. For I know and believe that whatever God has said will be fulfilled and will occur; not a single word of the prophecies will fail.'" (Tob 14:3–4bc, NRSVue)

**Reflection**: At the end of the OT (A) book of Tobit, Tobit expresses his belief to his son, Tobias, that prophesies taught to him will be fulfilled; however, to keep prophecies from failing, a teacher must teach people what they are. Written sometime in the third to second century BCE, the anonymous author of Tobit emphasizes that the readers of his novella believe that the divine prophetic words taught to them will be fulfilled. By the late 50s CE, Paul has separated the roles of teacher and prophet in his CB (NT) Letter to the Romans. He writes, ". . . [W]e, who are many, are one body in Christ, and individually we are members one of another. We have gifts that differ according to the grace given to us: prophecy, in proportion to faith; . . . the teacher, in teaching . . ."

(Rom 12:5–7, NRSVue); the gifts of prophecy and teacher are complementary. In the early 50s CE, he had written his First Letter to the Corinthians, in which he explained how God activates different gifts in different people as manifestations of the Spirit; he ranks the gifts as "first apostles, second prophets, third teachers" (1 Cor 12:28, NRSVue); earlier in the same letter he had written that the Spirit gives gifts for the common good, including prophecy (1 Cor 12:8, 10). In the second-generation Pauline letter—Ephesians—the author maintains the same order, except that he inserts evangelists and pastor before teachers (Eph 4:11). Paul tells the Corinthians to pursue love and the spiritual gifts that they might prophesy (1 Cor 14:1, 5). Later he adds that "prophecy is not for unbelievers but for believers" (1 Cor 12:22, NRSVue); "those who prophesy speak to other people for their upbuilding and encouragement and consolation" (1 Cor 14:3, NRSVue); "those who prophesy build up the church" (1 Cor 14:4, NRSVue); prophecy and teaching complement each other. Paul expresses his desire that he would like all the Corinthians to prophesy (1 Cor 14:5a), because, according to Paul's ranking, "[o]ne who prophesies is greater than one who speaks in tongues" (1 Cor 14:5b, NRSVue). By the end of the first century CE, there was a need for teachers to teach and for prophets to prophesy; that is why both prophets and teachers are found in the church in Antioch in the CB (NT) Acts of the Apostles (13:1). Many teachers were prophets, and many prophets were teachers.

**Meditation/Journal**: What important prophecy has been taught to you? Who was your prophetic teacher?

**Psalm Response**: [God,] "Oh! Teach us to live well! / Teach us to live wisely and well! / Surprise us with love at daybreak; / then we'll skip and dance all the day long. / And let the loveliness of our Lord, our God, rest on us, / confirming the work that we do. / Oh, yes, Affirm the work that we do." (Ps 90:12, 14, 17, TM)

## Uriah (Urijah)

**Scripture**: "There was another man prophesying in the name of the LORD, Uriah . . . . He prophesied against this city [Jerusalem] and against this land [of Judah] in words exactly like those of Jeremiah. And when King Jehoiakim . . . heard his words, the king sought to put him to death, but when Uriah heard of it, he was afraid and fled and escaped to Egypt. Then King Jehoiakim sent . . . men with him to Egypt, and they took Uriah from Egypt and brought him to King Jehoiakim, who struck him down with the sword and threw his dead body into the burial place of the common people." (Jer 26:20–23, NRSVue)

**Reflection**: In biblical literature, there are six men with the name of Uriah; however, only one of them is identified as a prophet during the reign of King Jehoiakim of Judah (608–597 BCE), only eleven years before King Nebuchadnezzar destroyed Jerusalem, captured all of Judah, and took every able-bodied man, woman, and child as captives of war to Babylon. In the HB (OT) book of Jeremiah, the prophet announced the word of the LORD: the Temple and Jerusalem were to be destroyed (Jer 26:1–15). As a result, some people were calling for Jeremiah's death. Some elders presented an example of what happened to the prophet Uriah after he spoke against the Temple and Jerusalem, just like Jeremiah had done. King Jehoiakim sent men to Egypt to find Uriah, who had fled there after prophesying, found him, brought him back to Jerusalem, and killed him. Ultimately, Uriah's words, just like Jeremiah's words, came true. In 586/587 BCE, King Nebuchadnezzar captured Jerusalem, demolished its walls, and burned the Temple, making Uriah a true prophet. The narrator of the story presents King Jehoiakim holding Uriah in contempt by killing him and burying his body in a common burial place. In other words, the king's judgment of Uriah was expected to serve as a warning to Jeremiah, but it only stiffened his resolve.

**Meditation/Journal**: Who has spoken a prophetic word to you that stiffened your resolve to continue on your course?

**Psalm Response**: "Alongside Babylon's rivers / we sat on the banks; we cried and cried, / remembering the good old days . . . . / Alongside the quaking aspens / we stacked our unplayed harps; / That's where our captors demanded songs, / sarcastic and mocking: / 'Sing us a happy . . . song!' / Oh, how could we ever sing GOD's song / in this wasteland? / If I ever forget you, Jerusalem, / let my fingers wither and fall off like leaves. / Let my tongue swell and turn black / if I fail to remember you, / If I fail, O dear Jerusalem, / to honor you as my greatest." (Ps 137:1–6, TM)

## Visions

**Scripture**: ". . . [T]he LORD came down in a pillar of cloud and stood at the entrance of the tent [of meeting] and called Aaron and Miriam, and they both came forward. And he said, 'Hear my words: When there are prophets among you, / I the LORD make myself known to them in visions; / I speak to them in dreams.'" (Num 12:5–6, NRSVue)

**Reflection**: Biblically, a vision is a supernatural experience in which God communicates with a person, while he or she is awake or asleep, either visually or auditorily or both. As recorded in the HB (OT) book of Numbers, the LORD explains that he makes himself known to prophets in visions. In the HB (OT) book of Genesis, the narrator states, "God spoke to Israel in visions of the night" (Gen 46:2, NRSVue). Through visions, which differ from dreams but may include dreams, God imparts special knowledge, guidance, or insight. Such special communications may reveal a future event, a truth, or guidance. In other words, visions are appearances of the LORD; they are revelations of the divine; they are spiritual experiences of the invisible God, yet present in a visible manner, like fire, smoke, or earthquake. In visions, ordinary objects take on prophetic significance; they help to transform an ordinary experience into an extraordinary one. The divine is mediated through a vision, and a message is delivered. While the HB (OT) book of Deuteronomy states, "Never since has there arisen a prophet in Israel like Moses, whom the LORD knew face to face" (Deut 34:10, NRSVue), in the CB (NT) gospel of John, the author presents Jesus telling Philip, "Whoever has seen me has seen the Father" (John 14:9b, NRSVue). Thus, not only is Jesus declared to be a prophet greater than Moses in the CB (NT), but he is an incarnate revelation of the LORD in his person; in other words, seeing Jesus is gazing on God. The Johannine Jesus is a vision of God.

**Meditation/Journal**: During your life, what special knowledge, guidance, or insight (vision) have you received from God? Explain.

**Psalm Response**: "A long time ago [, GOD,] you spoke in a vision, / you spoke to your faithful beloved: / 'I found David, my servant, / poured holy oil on his head . . . . / I'll guarantee his family tree / and underwrite his rule. / I've given my word, my whole and holy word; / do you think I would lie to David? / His family tree is here for good, / his sovereignty as sure as the sun, / Dependable as the phases of the moon, / inescapable as weather.'" (Ps 89:19a, 20, 29, 35–37, TM)

## Water

**Scripture**: ". . . Elijah took his mantle and rolled it up and struck the water [of the Jordan River]; the water was parted to the one side and to the other . . . . [Elisha] picked up the mantle of Elijah that had fallen from him and went back and stood on the bank of the Jordan. He took the mantle of Elijah that had fallen from him and struck the water . . . and the water was parted to the one side and to the other, and Elisha crossed over." (2 Kgs 2:8, 13–14, NRSVue)

**Reflection**: Some biblical prophets are known for their ability to part water so that a crossing can be made on dry ground. The prophet Moses is the first to stretch out his hand with his staff and divide the sea (Exod 14:16, 21, 26). It comes as no surprise when the people are thirsty in the wilderness and have no water to drink that Moses strikes a rock and water flows from it (Num 20:7, 9–11). Joshua, another prophet and Moses' successor as leader of the Israelites, divides the water of the Jordan River so the Israelites can cross on dry ground; when the priests carrying the ark, the sign of God's presence, step into the river, the water divides (Josh 3:8, 11, 13–17; 4:10–11). Thus, Joshua is depicted as a Moses-like character. Then, there are the prophets Elijah and Elisha. As noted in the Scripture text above, both use Elijah's mantel to strike the Jordan River, the water separates, and they cross and recross the Jordan River. In biblical literature, water represents chaos, which only God can control directly (Gen 1:6, 9; 6:17; 7:4, 10, 17, 21; 8:16) or through the prophets he sends to his people.

**Meditation/Journal**: What does water signify for you? Make a list.

**Psalm Response**: "After Israel left Egypt . . . / Judah became holy land for [GOD], / Israel the place of holy rule. / Sea took one look and ran the other way; / River Jordan turned around and ran off. / What's wrong with you, Sea, that you ran away? / and you, River Jordan, that you turned and ran off? / Tremble, Earth! You're in the Lord's presence! / in the presence of Jacob's God. / He turned the rock into a pool of cool water, / turned flint into fresh spring water." (Ps 114:1–3a, 5, 7–8, TM)

## Xerxes

**Scripture**: "When [Esther's messengers] told Mordecai what Esther had said, Mordecai told them to reply to Esther, 'Do not think that in the king's palace you will escape any more than all the other Jews. For if you keep silent at this time, relief and deliverance will rise for the Jews from another place, but you and your father's family will perish. Who knows? Perhaps you have come to royal dignity for just such a time as this.'" (Esth 4:12–14, NRSVue)

**Reflection**: The short story named the HB (OT) book of Esther with additional chapters in the OT (A) is set in the royal court of Persia. The king is Xerxes, also called Ahasuerus (Ezra 4:6) and Artaxerxes (Ezra 4:7; Add Esth 11:2a [A:2a]), who summons his Queen Vashti, who refuses to obey (Esth 1:10–22). Xerxes decides to dethrone Vashti and replace her with a new queen. Among the potential candidates is Esther, a Jewess, who has been raised by her uncle, Mordecai. The evil villain is Haman, who hatches a plot to kill all the Jews in the Persian realm. Because King Xerxes loves Esther (Esth 2:17), Mordecai urges her to go to him and plead for the life of the Jews. Esther knows that according to Persian law "if any man or woman [went] to the king inside the inner court without being called, [he or she was] to be put to death. Only if the king [held] out the golden scepter to someone may that person live" (Esth 4:11, NRSVue). Queen Esther hatches a plot to get to King Xerxes, destroy Haman, and rescue the Jews from genocide. While her uncle, Mordecai, is never called a prophet, the words he conveys to Esther are prophetic. He tells her what she needs to do, and she figures out how to do it.

**Meditation/Journal**: When have you listened to a prophetic figure and did what he or she said?

**Prayer Response**: "O my Lord, you alone are our king; help me, who am alone and have no helper but you, for my danger is in my hand. Ever since I was born I have heard . . . that you, O Lord, took Israel out of all the nations and our ancestors from among all their forebears for an everlasting inheritance and that you did for them all that you said. Remember, O Lord; make yourself known in this time of our affliction and give me courage, O King . . . . Put eloquent speech in my mouth . . . . But save us by your hand and help me, who am alone and have no helper but you, O Lord." (Add Esth 14:3–5, 12–14, TM)

## Years

**Scripture**: ". . . [T[hus says the LORD of hosts: . . . I am going to send for all the tribes of the north, says the LORD, even for King Nebuchadrezzar of Babylon, my servant, and I will bring them against this land and its inhabitants and against all these nations around; I will utterly destroy them . . . . This whole land shall become a ruin and a waste, and these nations shall serve the king of Babylon seventy years. Then after seventy years are completed, I will punish the king of Babylon and that nation . . . ." (Jer 25:8–9–12, NRSVue)

**Reflection**: The prophet Jeremiah receives a revelation from the LORD informing him that Babylon has been chosen as God's agent of destruction for Judah; the LORD refers to King Nebuchadrezzar as his servant. Once Nebuchadrezzar (Nebuchadnezzar) conquers Judah and Jerusalem, they will serve him for seventy years. Seventy is a sacred number formed from three plus four times ten. Three represents the spiritual (divine) order, and four represents the created order. Ten represents totality or a very long time. Thus, the exile is supposed to last a long time, according to Jeremiah; however, after fifty years, the LORD promises to punish Babylon. And so he does by raising up King Cyrus of Persia, who defeats the Babylonians and fulfills Jeremiah's words (2 Chr 36:22–23; Ezra 1:1). The prophet Isaiah refers to King Cyrus as his anointed—like a king of Judah—one he has called by name (Isa 44:28–45:13).

Thus, during the Jews' seventy (actually fifty) years of captivity in Babylon, the LORD employed the help of two non-Jewish kings to enact his will!

**Meditation/Journal**: In your life, who was the unlikely person chosen by God to minister to you in some way?

**Psalm Response**: "God, it seems you've been our home forever; / long before the mountains were born, / Long before you brought earth itself to birth . . . . / Patience! You've got all the time in the world—whether / a thousand years or a day, it's all the same to you. / We live for seventy years or so / (with luck we might make it to eighty) . . . . / Oh! Teach us to live well! / Teach us to live wisely and well!" (Ps 90:1–2a, 4, 10, 12, TM)

## Zechariah (father of John the Baptist)

**Scripture**: ". . . [T]here was as priest named Zechariah [who] was chosen by lot . . . to enter the sanctuary of the Lord to offer incense. . . . [T]here appeared to him an angel of the Lord, standing at the right side of the altar of incense. . . . [T]he angel said to him, 'Do not be afraid Zechariah, for your prayer has been heard. Your wife Elizabeth will bear you a son, and you will name him John. . . . [H]e will be great in the sight of the Lord; . . . even before his birth he will be filled with the Holy Spirit. With the spirit and power of Elijah he will go before him . . . to make ready a people prepared for the Lord. . . . [B]ecause you did not believe my words, which will be fulfilled in their time, you will become mute, unable to speak, until he day these things occur.'" (Luke 1:5, 9, 11, 13, 15, 17, 20, NRSVue)

**Reflection**: Zechariah, which means *God remembers*, is a popular biblical name; out of the twenty-eight men with the name Zechariah, there are three who are considered prophets. First, we have Zechariah, father of John the Baptist, who makes a unique appearance in Luke's Gospel (1:5–25; 57–79), only to disappear and never be mentioned again! This Zechariah is a priest (Luke 1:5), he is righteous (Luke 1:6), and the angel Gabriel (Luke 1:19)—meaning *God is Strong*—appeared to him in the Lord's sanctuary, where he was offering incense (Luke 1:11) and told him that he and his wife Elizabth, both in their older years, would have a son (Luke 1:13), and he, like Samuel before him, would never drink wine or strong drink (Luke 1:15) (Nazarite), but he would be filled with the Holy Spirit—the author of Luke's Gospel's way of marking Pentecost before it happens in the Acts of the Apostles. The role of John was to prepare people for the Lord. Because Zechariah asked the angel how all this was to happen, he was struck mute (Luke 1:20), but after John is born (Luke 1:57), circumcised (Luke 1:59), and named (Luke 1:60–63), Zechariah's muteness is removed—the angel's words are fulfilled—and he can speak (Luke 1:64). Then, like prophets before him, "Zechariah was filled with the Holy Spirit and prophesied" (Luke 1:67).

**Meditation/Journal**: During your life, what sign, like Zechariah's muteness, have you received?

**Canticle Response**: ". . . [Y]ou, my child, 'Prophet of the Highest,' / will go ahead of the Master to prepare his ways, / Present the offer of salvation to his people, / the forgiveness of their sins. / Through the heartfelt mercies of our God, / God's Sunrise will break in upon us, / Shining on those in the darkness, / those sitting in the shadow of death, / Then showing us the way, one foot at a time, / down the path of peace." (Luke 1:76–79, TM)

## Zechariah (son of Berechiah)

**Scripture**: ". . . [T]he word of the LORD came to the prophet Zechariah son of Berechiah . . . , saying: 'Thus says the LORD of hosts: Return to me, says the LORD of hosts, and I will return to you, says the LORD of hosts. Do not be like your ancestors, to whom the former prophets proclaimed, "Thus says the LORD of hosts . . . ." But they did not hear or heed me, says the LORD. Your ancestors, where are they? And the prophets, do they live forever?'" (Zech 1:1–5, NRSVue)

**Reflection**: As already noted above, Zechariah is a popular biblical name; out of the twenty-eight men with the name Zechariah, there are three who are considered prophets. The second of the three is Zechariah, son of Berechiah (Zech 1:1). This Zechariah writes to those Jews who had returned from Babylonian exile and found Judah and Jerusalem in ruins. He begins his book by reminding the returned exiles that the LORD was angry with their ancestors (Zech 1:2). Then, speaking for the LORD, he invites those who have returned to Judah and Jerusalem to return to the LORD, who will, in turn, return to them. He advises them not to be stubborn, like their ancestors, who died in Babylonian captivity, or the prophets, who have passed from the scene. The original book consisted of eight visions (Zech 1:7–6:8) with words of hope emphasizing God's control of history: "Thus says the LORD: I will return . . . and dwell in the midst of Jerusalem; Jerusalem shall be called the faithful city and the mountain of the LORD of hosts shall be called the holy mountain" (Zech 8:3, NRSVue). At a later time, two prophetic collections were appended to Zechariah—chapters 9 through 11 and 12 through 14; they differ in style and content and came from another prophetic figure or group. Because the land and Jerusalem lay in ruins, the future did not look bright for the exiles who had returned. Zechariah attempted to instill hope and to urge the returnees to begin the process of rebuilding their cities and their lives.

**Meditation/Journal**: Who has given you hope, when you needed to rebuild your life or a part of your life? Explain.

**Psalm Response**: "Tell me, what's going on, GOD? / How long do I have to live? / Give me the bad news! / Oh, we're all puffs of air. / Oh! We're all shadows in a campfire. / Oh! we're just spit in the wind. / We make our pile, and then we leave it. / What am I doing in the meantime, Lord? / *Hoping*, that's what I'm doing—hoping / You'll save me . . . . / I'll say no more, I'll shut my mouth, / since you, Lord, are behind all this." (Ps 39:4, 5b–8a, 9, TM)

## Zechariah (son of Jehoida)

**Scripture**: ". . . [The] spirit of God took possession of Zechariah son of the priest Jehoida; he stood above the people and said to them, 'Thus says God: Why do you transgress the commandments of the LORD, so that you cannot prosper? Because you have forsaken the LORD, he has also forsaken you.' But they conspired against him, and by command of the king they stoned him to death in the court of the house of the LORD. King Joash did not remember the kindness that Jehoida, Zechariah's father, had shown him but killed his son. As he was dying, he said, 'May the Lord see and avenge!'" (2 Chr 24:20–22, NRSVue)

**Reflection**: As mentioned twice above, Zechariah is a popular biblical name; out of the twenty-eight men with the name Zechariah, there are three who are considered prophets. The third of the three is Zechariah, son of the priest Jehoida (2 Chr 24:2) during the reign of King Joash of Judah (835–796 BCE). According to the chronicler, after Jehoida died, the officials of Judah "abandoned the house of the LORD, the God of their ancestors, and served the sacred poles and the idols" (2 Chr 24:18, NRSVue). The LORD "sent prophets among them to bring them back to the LORD; they testified against them, but they would not listen," states the chronicler (2 Chr 24:19, NRSVue). It is a story told over and over again in many biblical books! However, Jehoida's son, Zechariah, was seized by God's spirit and told all that they had abandoned the LORD, who had abandoned them, because of their devotion to idols. In other words, Zechariah merely repeated what the prophets before him had said. And just as the prophets before him were killed, Zechariah was stoned in the temple square with King Joash's permission. As the chronicler made clear, the king had forgotten all that Zechariah's father, Jehoida, had done for him; because he had forgotten, he became an accomplice in murder. The LORD saw and avenged Zechariah's murder, according to the chronicler, by delivering Judah into the hand of Aram "because [Judah] had abandoned the LORD, the God of their ancestors" (2 Chr 24:24, NRSVue). Also, King Joash's servants conspired against him "because of the blood of the son of the priest Jehoida, and they killed him on his bed" (2 Chr 24:25, NRSVue). Thus, the prophet Zechariah's words—"May the LORD see and avenge!" (2 Chr 24:22b)—were fulfilled.

**Meditation/Journal**: In your lifetime, where have you witnessed the LORD seeing and avenging the death of a prophet? Explain.

**Psalm Response**: "GOD, put an end to evil; / avenging God, show your colors! / Judge of the earth, take your stand; / throw the book at the arrogant. / GOD, the wicked get away with murder— / how long will you let this go on? / They brag and boast / and crow about their crimes! / They walk all over your people, GOD, / exploit and abuse your precious people. / They take out anyone who gets in their way; / if they can't use them, they kill them. / They think, 'GOD isn't looking, / . . . God is out to lunch.'" (Ps 93:1–7, TM)

## Zedekiah

**Scripture**: Thus says the LORD: ". . . [A]ll you exiles whom I sent away from Jerusalem to Babylon, hear the word of the LORD: Thus says the LORD of hosts, the God of Israel, concerning . . . Zedekiah . . . , who [is] prophesying a lie to you in my name; I am going to deliver [him] into the hand of King Nebuchadrezzar of Babylon, and he shall kill [him] before your eyes. And on account of [him] this curse shall be used by all the exiles from Judah in Babylon: 'The LORD make you like Zedekiah . . . , whom the king of Babylon roasted in the fire,' because [he has] perpetrated outrage in Israel . . . and [has] spoken in my name lying words that I did not command [him] . . . .'" (Jer 29:20–23, NRSVue)

**Reflection**: According to the prophet Jeremiah, there were false prophets among the Jewish exiles in Babylon. Through Jeremiah, the LORD had declared that the exiles would be in Babylon for seventy years (Jer 29:10). However, false prophets had said that their exile would not last as long as Jeremiah had prophesied. One of those false prophets was Zedekiah, son of Maaseiah (Jer 29:21). Jeremiah wrote to the exiles and told them that Zedekiah was full of words that did not come from the LORD. Therefore, any exile acclaiming Zedekiah would soon be using his name in a curse, because the LORD was delivering him into King Nebuchadnezzar's hand for execution for supporting an uprising against him. Zedekiah's name would be used in a curse, after the king roasted him in fire! Jeremiah demonstrates his absolute confidence in the power of the LORD's words to get rid of the false prophet Zedekiah and remove the false news that the exiles thought they had heard!

**Meditation/Journal**: Who has delivered false news to you? Explain.

**Psalm Response**: "Listen, GOD, I'm calling at the top of my lungs: / 'Be good to me! Answer me!' / You've always been right there for me; / don't turn your back on me now / Don't throw me out, don't abandon me; / you've always kept the door open. / Point me down your highway, GOD; / direct me along a well-lighted street . . . . / Don't throw me to the dogs, / those liars who are out to get me, / filling the air with their threats." (Ps 27:7, 9, 11–12, TM)

## Zephaniah

**Scripture**: "The word of the LORD that came to Zephaniah . . . in the days of King Josiah . . . . I will utterly sweep away everything / from the face of the earth, says the LORD. / I will stretch out my hand against Judah / and against all the inhabitants of Jerusalem, / and I will cut off from this place every remnant of Baal / and the name of the idolatrous priests . . . . / Be silent before the Lord GOD, / for the day of the LORD is at hand!" (Zeph 1:1–2, 4, 7, NRSVue)

**Reflection**: Zephaniah's HB (OT) book consists of three chapters printed on three pages in many Bibles. While he doesn't have a lot to write about, the words he uses are filled with fire! He presents the LORD destroying everything on the face of the earth—reminiscent of the story of Noah in the HB (OT) book of Genesis. All was to be desolate in Judah and Jerusalem. The King of Judah is Josiah (640–608 BCE). The fall of the Northern Kingdom of Israel to Assyria was on the horizon (722 BCE), and the fall of the Southern Kingdom of Judah was not too far away (586/587 BCE); Zephaniah refers to the fall of Judah and Jerusalem as "the day of the LORD" (Zeph 1:7a, NRSVue). The issue, as far as the LORD is concerned, is idolatry, specifically the worship of Baal. Zephaniah's call for silence before God was a hope that the people of Judah and Jerusalem would listen to what he spoke in the name of the LORD and repent. Once he finished describing the horrors that the LORD was visiting upon Judah and Jersualem, he offered a few words about leaving a remnant, who would seek refuge in God (Zeph 3:11–20).

**Meditation/Journal**: In your life, who has spoken words of horror and destruction to you? What did he or she say? How did you respond?

**Canticle Response**: ". . . [S]ing, Daughter Zion! / Raise the rafters, Israel! / Daughter Jerusalem, / be happy! celebrate! / GOD has reversed his judgments against you / and sent your enemies off chasing their tails. / From now on, GOD is Israel's king, / in charge at the center. / There's nothing to fear from evil / ever again! / Your GOD is present among you . . . ." (Zeph 3:14–15, 17a, TM)

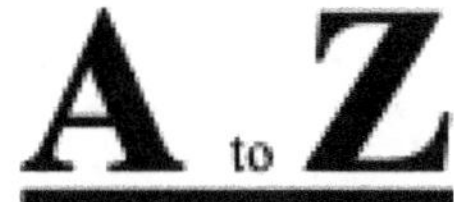



# A to Z

# Bibliography

*New Revised Standard Version Updated Edition and Apocryphal/Deuterocanonical Books of the Old Testament*. Grand Rapids, MI: Zondervan, 2022.

Peters, Ellis. *The Summer of the Danes*. New York, NY: Mysterious, 1991.

Peterson, Eugene H., William Griffin, trans. *The Message: Catholic/Ecumenical Edition, The Bible in Contemporary Language*. Chicago, IL: ACTA, 2013.

## Recent Books by Mark G. Boyer Published by Wipf & Stock

*Nature Spirituality: Praying with Wind, Water, Earth, Fire*

*A Spirituality of Ageing*

*Weekday Saints: Reflections on Their Scriptures*

*Human Wholeness: A Spirituality of Relationship*

*A Simple Systematic Mariology*

*Praying Your Way through Luke's Gospel and the Acts of the Apostles*

*An Abecedarian of Animal Spirit Guides: Spiritual Growth through Reflections on Creatures*

*Overcome with Paschal Joy: Chanting through Lent and Easter—Daily Reflections with Familiar Hymns*

*Taking Leave of Your Home: Moving in the Peace of Christ*

*An Abecedarian of Sacred Trees: Spiritual Growth through Reflections on Woody Plants*

*Divine Presence: Elements of Biblical Theophanies*

*Fruit of the Vine: A Biblical Spirituality of Wine*

*Names for Jesus: Reflections for Advent and Christmas*

*Talk to God and Listen to the Casual Reply: Experiencing the Spirituality of John Denver*

*Christ Our Passover Has Been Sacrificed: A Guide through Paschal Mystery Spirituality—Mystical Theology in* The Roman Missal

*Rosary Primer: The Prayers, The Mysteries, and the New Testament*

*From Contemplation to Action: The Spiritual Process of Divine Discernment Using Elijah and Elisha as Models*

## Recent Books by Mark G. Boyer Published by Wipf & Stock

*Love Addict*

*All Things Mary: Honoring the Mother of God—An Anthology of Marian Reflections*

*Shhh! The Sound of Sheer Silence: A Biblical Spirituality that Transforms*

*What is Born of the Spirit is Spirit: A Biblical Spirituality of Spirit*

*Very Short Reflections—for Advent and Christmas, Lent and Easter, Ordinary Time, and Saints—through the Liturgical Year*

*Living Parables: Today's Versions*

*My Life of Ministry, Writing, Teaching, and Traveling: The Autobiography of an Old Mines Missionary*

*300 Years of the French in Old Mines: A Narrative History of the Oldest Village in Missouri*

*Journey into God: Spiritual Reflections for Travelers*

*Monthly Entries for the Spiritual but not Religious through the Year: Texts, Reflections, Journal/Meditations, and Prayers for the Spiritual but not Religious*

*The Shelbydog Chronicles by Shelby Cole as Recorded by Mark G. Boyer: A Novel*

*Four Catholic Pioneers in Missouri: Lamarque, Kenrick, Fox, and Hogan: Irish Missionaries and Their Supporter*

*Smothered with Inexhaustible Mercy: An Anthology of Poems*

*Spirituality for the Solitary: A Handbook for Those Who Live Alone*

*Seasons of Biblical Spirituality: Spring, Summer, Autumn, Winter*

*Biblical Names for God: An Abecedarian Anthology of Spiritual Reflections for Anytime*

*More Shelbydog Chronicles: Reflections on a Dog's Life by Her Friend, Knowing Your Pet*

*His Mercy Endures Forever: Biblical Reflections on Divine Mercy for Anytime*

*The Roman Catholic Lectionary and the Bible: Analysis, Conclusions, Suggested Alternatives*

*The Spirit of the Lord God: Biblical Names and Images for the Holy Spirit; An Abecedarian Anthology of Spiritual Reflections for Anytime*

*A Biblical Morning & Evening Prayer Manual: A Modern Book of Hours, Ways to Begin and End the Day*

## Recent Books by Mark G. Boyer Published by Wipf & Stock

*The Folks in the Woods: A Memoir of Brown Hollow, Missouri, 1874–1991*

*The Liturgical Environment: What the Documents Say about Roman Catholic Churches, Fourth Edition, Updated and Revised*

*Eavesdropping on Paul: Reading Others' Biblical Mail*

*Biblical Creation Stories: Plural Ways to Nourish Spirituality*

*Living with Grace: John Denver Spirituality in Song and Word: An Abecedarian of Themes*

*Spiritual Oxygen: Biblical Spirituality for the 21st Century*

*Final Shelbydog Chronicles: Touched by a Dog*

www.ingramcontent.com/pod-product-compliance
Lightning Source LLC
LaVergne TN
LVHW020640100826
845148LV00012B/2259
* 9 7 9 8 3 8 5 2 6 6 5 8 6 *